"Jonathan truly understands youth and how to minister to them. He also knows how to communicate Scripture to youth in high-impact ways. that do exactly that."

—**Dan Kimball, author,** *They Like Jesus but Not the Chu*

"Don't make the mistake of thinking this is another book of quickie ideas for microwave youth work: 10 minutes of prep time and 10 minutes of mush that has about 10 minutes of impact in a student's life! What Jonathan has given us in *10-Minute Talks* is a collection of engaging, biblical messages that can be delivered in 10 minutes—but also offer students images and examples that can provide a lifetime of impact. I also really like the extra touches provided with each talk: The transition helps, the specific biblical passages, the application ideas, the presentation tips. For me, those are some of toughest parts of message preparation. I know a lot of youth workers will find this book really helpful. Good stuff!"

—**Duffy Robbins, author,** *Speaking to Teenagers*; **professor of youth ministry, Eastern University**

"Good, tight talks to teenagers are a challenge, if not an art form. Jonathan's book not only supplies practical outlines and stories that make this task much easier, it teaches a way of thinking about talks that you'll carry with you into a fruitful ministry anywhere. While there's no such thing as a 'just add water' resource, if you learn to 'just add context,' this book will jump on and off your shelf like your favorite cereal!"

—**Dr. Dave Rahn, vice president and chief ministry officer, Youth for Christ/USA**

"Working with junior highers, I've learned the importance of short, high-impact lessons. Thanks, Jonathan, for providing us with an easy-to-use resource that makes the tough job of writing talks a whole lot easier!"

—**Kurt Johnston, Saddleback Church; author,** *My Faith, My Family, My Friends,* **and** *My School* **(from the Youth Specialties Middle School Survival Series)**

"It seems as though books about how to do 'talks' are a dime a dozen. Not this one. *10-Minute Talks* is full of material that flat out works. If you're a youth worker who'd rather spend time ministering to students than Googling the latest lesson outlines and illustrations, *10-Minute Talks* is exactly what you need. Jonathan's talks combine compelling intros, solid biblical teaching, and practical applications. You won't be disappointed!"

—**Greg Stier, president, Dare 2 Share Ministries**

"If you can talk to kids, you can talk to anybody! I've always believed that youth pastors make the best preachers, and Jonathan's book proves the point. His method and messages will help every communicator connect quickly, communicate clearly, and close effectively."

—**F. Bryan Wilkerson, senior pastor, Grace Chapel, Lexington, Massachusetts**

"What should busy youth workers do with a book that will help them connect better and speak better—while actually saving time? Buy it and use it! Jonathan McKee has taken a lifetime of speaking experience and put it into 24 great messages that you can actually use! This is no ivory-tower collection of lectures that someone hopes *might* connect; no, the illustrations are sharp, the messages relevant, and the content is tested and proven. If you have the gift of teaching, but your kids don't seem to have the gift of listening, *10-Minute Talks* could be for you!"

—**Ray Johnston, senior pastor, Bayside Church, Granite Bay, California**

"Few things have greater power than a story. Jonathan McKee has gathered some unforgettable stories that can provide a foundation for presenting life-changing truth. If you only have 10 minutes, this may be what you need to make every one of them count."

—**Ken Davis, author, *How to Speak to Youth...and Keep Them Awake at the Same Time***

"Spurgeon said that the first golden rule in holding an audience's attention is to say something worth hearing. *Relevance.* That's what keeps people riveted on the Word of God. Jonathan McKee shows us how to demonstrate the Bible's relevance for youth. These talks grew in the soil of Jonathan's experience (young people have real needs) and were forged in the fire of his convictions (the Bible has real answers)."

—**Jeffrey Arthurs, professor of preaching and communication, Gordon-Conwell Theological Seminary**

"Jonathan does two things well here: At the beginning of almost every talk he grabs hold of his listeners' ears and commands their attention. Then, through the use of story and thoughtful transitions, he invites them to allow God to change either their attitudes or their behavior."

—**Joel Eidsness, pastor emeritus, Walnut Hill Community Church, Bethel, Connecticut**

"Jonathan McKee has brought another outstanding resource to the youth ministry world. Our YouTube and Facebook culture demands instant answers that are entertaining, as well as relevant. In *10-Minute Talks*, Jonathan shows just how to get the job done. The talks are relevant, powerful, and perfect for just about any youth setting."

—**Jay Laffoon, cofounder, Celebrate Your Marriage Conferences®**

JONATHAN MCKEE

10-MINUTE TALKS

24 Messages Your Students Will Love

JONATHAN MCKEE

10-MINUTE TALKS

24 Messages Your Students Will Love

 ZONDERVAN®

 ZONDERVAN.com/
AUTHORTRACKER
follow your favorite authors

 youth
specialties

YOUTH SPECIALTIES

10-Minute Talks: 24 Messages Your Students Will Love
Copyright 2008 by Jonathan McKee

Youth Specialties resources, 300 S. Pierce St., El Cajon, CA 92020 are published by Zondervan, 5300 Patterson Ave. SE, Grand Rapids, MI 49530.

Library of Congress Cataloging-in-Publication Data

McKee, Jonathan R. (Jonathan Ray), 1970-
  10-minute talks : 24 messages your students will love / Jonathan McKee.
    p. cm.
  ISBN 978-0-310-27494-0 (pbk.)
  1. Church work with teenagers. I. Title. II. Title: Ten minute talks.
  BV4447.M236 2008
  268'.67—dc22   2008026363

All Scripture quotations, unless otherwise indicated, are taken from the *Holy Bible, Today's New International Version™*. TNIV®. Copyright 2001, 2005 by International Bible Society. Used by permission of Zondervan. All rights reserved.

Any Internet addresses (websites, blogs, etc.) and telephone numbers printed in this book are offered as a resource. They are not intended in any way to be or imply an endorsement by Youth Specialties, nor does Youth Specialties vouch for the content of these sites and numbers for the life of this book.

Cover design by SharpSeven Design
Interior design by Mark Novelli, IMAGO MEDIA

Printed in the United States of America

09 10 11 12 13 14 • 20 19 18 17 16 15 14 13 12 11 10 9 8 7 6 5 4 3

ACKNOWLEDGMENTS

Someone recently told me, "You the man!" When I hear that, I can only respond, "Nope, but I know him." God deserves the credit. When you enjoy parts of this book, that's where God was doing the work. If you don't like something in the book, then it was probably just me.

My dad deserves more than just an acknowledgment in this book—his name should probably be on the cover with mine. He helped me with so much of the research that went into these stories and was a great help with many of the wrap-ups. Thanks, Dad.

Much love to my wife, Lori, and my three kids, Alec, Alyssa, and Ashley.

Thank you to all those who partner with our ministry, The Source for Youth Ministry.

And a big shout out to all my friends who provided me with ideas, feedback, and final tweaks. Thanks to Todd, KJ, Lane, Danette, TJ, Mikey, Furby, and Brian.

CONTENTS

Section Two: Outreach Talks (listed by title / topic)

WHY **10** MINUTES?

Have you ever stood in front of a few hundred teenagers who didn't really want to listen to you? Oh, it's not like they have anything personal against you. Honestly, they'd just rather play a game or talk with the cutest guy or girl in the room than sit and listen to you give a talk.

So how do you get their attention?

Better yet, how do you *keep* their attention?

When I first started in ministry I ran an outreach program on a junior high campus. We regularly used crazy icebreakers, fun activities, and creative discussions. But our hope was to provide more than just fun and games. We wanted to share truth with them.

The crowd was tough. I learned right away that attention spans were short. I knew that whenever I stood in front of a group, I had only a few seconds to grab their attention. Even more challenging, I had less than 10 minutes to make my point. Before long I was spending a lot of time developing effective 10-minute talks.

Many of us find ourselves with the same need. Have you ever programmed a church event where the evening is planned perfectly, but there's no time for a full-blown sermon? For one reason or another the evening calls for a short talk or a wrap-up—maybe just 10 minutes or less. What can you do in 10 minutes or less?

My friend Andy ran a skateboard ministry that drew hundreds of kids. He made a deal with them: They could skate for an hour, then break for 10 minutes and listen to him share something, then skate for

20 more minutes. Every week Andy planned a talk that was less than 10 minutes. Even if he brought a special speaker—10 minutes.

My friend Omar used to play basketball after school with a group of high school students. Each week they'd come to a neighborhood court and play, and each week Omar would break for halftime and share with them for less than 10 minutes. Omar was always looking for *10-minute talk ideas.*

So what do you do when you only have 10 minutes (or less) to make your point?

Youth ministry regularly consists of moments when a short talk is the perfect solution. No three points and a poem and no long fancy outlines—just a 10-minute talk that makes a single point loud and clear through a powerful story.

All the aforementioned youth programs began using the 10-minute talk as their teaching tool—basically a story relevant to the topic of discussion. And it was the only up-front teaching for the entire evening. One story—one clear point.

My hope is that this book will provide you with what I'm always on the lookout for—a nice little collection of short talks or sermons. Today, many youth workers don't leave a lot of time for the talk. The increasing popularity of small groups and lengthy activities often means you only have about 10 minutes to wrap up the evening with a talk or story. This book provides just that.

10-MINUTE TIPS
HOW TO USE THIS BOOK

How exactly do you make a point in 10 minutes?

Stories are powerful teaching tools. I'm sure you don't need convincing to use the same method Jesus used in his teaching. Stories are relevant, they paint pictures, and they hold the attention of the toughest crowds. Some of the best talks I've heard have been one story with one point—and one powerful impact.

That's the goal of this book.

Each of these 10-minute talks includes one story teaching one clear point, using one main passage of Scripture. Some may be a little shorter than 10 minutes and some a minute or two longer. You can adapt them as necessary. (That's why we included the handy little supplemental CD in the back of the book—to provide you the freedom to customize all the talks as you prepare to give them.) And who knows—these talks might even spark memories of stories from your own life you can use instead, which is even better!

The talks are divided into two sections:

1. **Spiritual Growth Talks**—for teenagers who already have relationships with Christ but need to grow in their faith.
2. **Outreach Talks**—for teenagers who don't know Christ and need to hear the gospel message.

Each talk provides you with several elements:

Title

Topic

Big Idea: The one point the talk communicates, usually in the form of a sound bite.

Scripture: The passage of Scripture you'll use.

Particulars: Specifics about the story in this talk, such as background and even hints on how to tell it (if the talk is unusually short or long I'll indicate it here).

The Story: The bulk of the talk.

Transition Statement: Helps you segue from the story to the Big Idea (you'll want to rehearse this—good transition statements carry your audience smoothly through to the Big Idea).

Application and Scripture: Verbalizing the Big Idea and sharing the scriptural foundation.

Closing: Concluding statement, application, and prayer or call to respond.

Don't let all the categories scare you. Using these, you'll gain the essentials to tell a memorable story and bring home a biblical truth loudly and clearly.

(Note: The supplemental CD also includes a complete small group curriculum that corresponds with each talk!)

FOUR SIMPLE TIPS TO HELP YOU EFFECTIVELY USE THESE TALKS

1. **Memorize the talk.**

   Don't worry—you don't have to memorize it word for word. Think of the talk as a joke you just heard. How many times have you heard someone tell a joke, and the next day you turned around and told it to someone else? Memorize these talks just like that.

   In many situations you won't need every detail—just the main story line. For example, *Save Me!* is about a guy who gets trapped on a desert island. You could probably read or hear this talk once and then turn around and present it flawlessly. The details aren't that important—you can even change them up a bit.

   But other talks, such as the life story of Tom Brady (*More Than This*), might take more effort to memorize because of the stats. We don't want to invent history! *The American Dream— or Was It?* includes a bunch of statistics about lottery winners. I tell this story without notes and then pull out the statistics and read them at the end.

   The point of memorization is to free yourself from the handcuffs of notes, allowing your story to flow naturally.

2. Practice the talk out loud at least once.

I'm recommending this as a bare minimum. I rehearse these stories numerous times to perfect my transitions and get a feel for my own timing. One person did a trial run of one of these talks, and it took him just eight minutes. Another guy giving the same talk took 20 minutes (he really stretched it out).

Many of these talks have that flexibility. You might conclude that some stories carry too many details, so be flexible there. If you like details, use them. But feel free to omit statistics, scores, years, and average wind speed if those details seem superfluous.

Bottom line: Evaluate your needs, consider your time limitations, and adjust accordingly. Be aware that it's practicing these talks out loud that gives you these options.

3. Master your landmarks.

I always tell the speakers I train, "Make sure you have a captivating beginning, polished transitions, and a powerful ending." If you're in a rush and you decide to skip practicing these talks out loud (which, again, I don't recommend), then at least practice your first three lines, your transition statement, and your closing. The other details can settle into this framework.

4. Bathe it in prayer.

Don't try to do it alone. God doesn't need our help to change lives, but God has allowed us to be part of the process. So don't leave God out of it.

SECTION ONE:
SPIRITUAL GROWTH TALKS

TALK 01

TITLE: WHO'S IN YOUR BACK SEAT?

TOPIC: Friends

BIG IDEA: Be careful who you hang out with.

SCRIPTURE:

> "Wisdom will save you from the ways of wicked men, from men whose words are perverse, who have left the straight paths to walk in dark ways, who delight in doing wrong and rejoice in the perverseness of evil, whose paths are crooked and who are devious in their ways." (Proverbs 2:12-15)

PARTICULARS:

This true story took place in Sacramento. It'll get kids thinking not only about who they hang out with but also about choices and consequences.

THE STORY:

Chitho never could've predicted how the morning would end. This 16-year-old never realized that his decision to give someone a ride would be fatal.

It started with a simple car ride. Chitho picked up Saul and José. Music pumping, the boys drove to Hallie's and picked her up, then continued across town.

Their first stop was for gas. Hallie, a teenage mother, wanted to pick up her son at her mom's house. Someone else wanted to go to Wal-Mart, but the four teenagers decided to eat first.

They stopped at McDonald's for burgers and ate in the car.

Chitho, the driver, was 19 years old and had never been in trouble with the law. Saul, 19, rode beside him, with José and 18-year-old Hallie in the back seat. Jose had been released just three weeks before from Boys Ranch, a Sacramento County facility for repeat juvenile offenders.

After the burger break they resumed their trip to Wal-Mart. Along the way, a teenager stood alone at a bus stop.

That's when it started.

José told Chitho to pull over. "Let's check out this kid and see what he has," he said.

At this point Chitho made a decision that changed the lives of every person in the car—a decision that resulted in his death, the incarceration of two others, and numerous sleepless nights for many involved. Chitho turned the car around and parked near the bus stop.

José grabbed a fake gun that looked pretty real and popped out of the back seat. Hallie objected, "This is stupid! I gotta go!" But José wouldn't back down.

Saul got out with José, and together they walked over to the bus stop and robbed the kid. They ran back to the car, and Chitho drove off.

José began asking to go to other places; Hallie just begged to go home. But Chitho continued on to Wal-Mart with his fellow felony offenders.

Pulling into Wal-Mart, they passed a police car. When they parked, another police car parked near them.

Officer Kevin Howland walked up to Chitho's car and began questioning them. The robbery at the bus stop just three minutes prior had already been called in, and a car that looked like Chitho's had been reported fleeing the scene. Officer Howland was following up the call.

The conversation didn't go well. Officer Howland asked if they had any weapons.

Chitho couldn't believe it had come to this. He didn't know the legalities. *Accessory? Guilty by association?* He didn't know what the charge would be, but he knew he was in trouble.

Chitho wasn't innocent—he was the one driving the car. He was the one who made the U-turn at the bus stop. Even though he didn't know what the consequences of the U-turn would be, in the very moment he made the turn Chitho probably knew he was making the wrong decision.

And now he was reaping the consequences of that decision. A police officer was at his window and the situation was getting out of hand.

"Let's go! Let's go! Let's go!" José barked from behind Chitho.

Chitho couldn't think. He knew he was in trouble. Maybe they *could* get away. Maybe, even now, he could still avoid getting into trouble.

"Let's go! Let's go! Let's go!"

And that's when it happened.

Chitho slammed the car in reverse, hitting the rear passenger side of Howland's vehicle. Police reported that the impact pushed the cruiser a few feet across the parking lot.

That's when everything went crazy.

Officer Howland drew his gun. Chitho put the car in drive and stepped on the gas. Police reported that Chitho's car would've sandwiched Officer Howland between two cars if he hadn't jumped on the hood.

Officer Howland fired eight rounds into the car.

Glass shattered as the shots rang out. The Chrysler crashed into a palm tree near the entrance of the shopping center.

Silence.

Chitho was dead.

Anyone in the car that day would tell you Chitho wasn't the instigator. Chitho wasn't a troublemaker. Chitho didn't rob anyone, and he definitely wasn't trying to kill anyone.

But Chitho made several mistakes that day behind the wheel, and his last mistake cost him his life. Chitho died of gunshot wounds to the chest and right arm.

One bullet made it past Chitho and hit José in the wrist. People who knew the situation probably would've said that the bullets hit the wrong person that day.

Hallie was released one day after the incident. The next day Saul was arraigned in Sacramento Superior Court on felony charges of robbery and receiving stolen property from the boy they robbed at the bus stop. José faced similar charges, and even though he was 16, he was prosecuted as an adult.

But Chitho wouldn't live to face any charges. Chitho's decisions that morning were his last.

They say hindsight is 20/20. You wonder: If Chitho had been given a second chance to think through his first decision that morning—would he have picked up José?

Would you?

TRANSITION STATEMENT:

Who are you letting in your back seat?

Who are you surrounding yourself with?

Chitho was a good kid. But on that particular morning, he surrounded himself with bad company. That one decision led to other bad decisions that ultimately cost him his life.

Think about choices. Chitho made a series of choices that day:

> a choice to pick up José and Saul,
> a choice to go driving around with them instead of just heading home,
> a choice to make a U-turn and let his passengers start trouble with a stranger,
> a choice to continue driving them after they committed a crime,
> and the choice to run from a police officer.

Chitho made most of these choices with someone barking in his ear. If José hadn't been barking in his ear, he probably wouldn't have made the choices he did.

Who's barking in your ear?

APPLICATION AND SCRIPTURE:

Be careful who you let in your back seat. Be careful who you listen to.

The Bible consistently talks about the importance of surrounding ourselves with those who will build us up, and being careful to avoid those who will lead us away from what's right. Check out this excerpt from the book of Proverbs in the Bible:

> "Wisdom will save you from the ways of wicked men, from men whose words are perverse, who have left the straight paths to walk in dark ways, who delight in doing wrong and rejoice in the perverseness of evil, whose paths are crooked and who are devious in their ways" (Proverbs 2:12-15).

God gives us the wisdom to watch out for people like this. He also reminds us in other passages (such as Hebrews 10:25) to surround ourselves with other believers, encouraging each other in doing what's right.

Who do you surround yourself with?

Are you careful who you let in your back seat?

CLOSING:

Some of us probably need to rethink some of the people we surround ourselves with.

I'm going to close with prayer. I challenge you, as each of you bows your head and closes your eyes, to think for a moment in silence. Think about *yourself* for a few moments, not those around you.

Some of you, as you sit there in silence, know that you have people in your life who are dragging you down. They might not be as bad as the kids in the story, but you know in your heart that they don't desire what's right and what's true. Maybe you need to avoid hanging out with some of these people. I'm not saying you can't be nice to them in the hallways at school, but let's be honest—we have the choice who we allow ourselves to spend time with. We need to surround ourselves with people who encourage us to do what's right instead of people who drag us down.

Let's pray together about this. You can pray with me silently:

Sample Prayer: *God, you know who it is that I've allowed into my life—my back seat, for lack of a better term. You know that I've probably even been influenced by them to do wrong. It's clear you don't like that. Forgive me, God. But more than that, help me to steer clear of this kind of trouble. Give me even just one or two people who stand for what's right and true—people who make you a priority in their lives. Give me some of these people in my life.*

God, I give you my friends. In Jesus' name, Amen.

Source: "Passenger describes Natomas shooting: Woman says slain driver didn't try to hit officer," by Crystal Carreon and Christina Jewett, staff writers, *Sacramento Bee*, Thursday, May 25, 2006.

TALK 02
TITLE: IT'S ME

TOPIC: Compassion

BIG IDEA: Only through Jesus can we have the strength to love the unlovable.

SCRIPTURE:

> "The King will reply, 'Truly I tell you, whatever you did for one of the least of these brothers and sisters of mine, you did for me.'" (Matthew 25:40)

PARTICULARS:

I wrote a fictional story based on a true situation that happened to one of my ministry friends. Her story inspired me and has inspired many others.

THE STORY:

There was something almost supernatural about Kristen. When circumstances were the toughest, she was the strongest. When conditions were bleak, she maintained hope. When everyone else was despondent, Kristen brought an aroma of joy to the room.

Anyone who met her thought that she was probably an angel. But Kristen was quite human. She was as real as anyone you've ever met. She liked ice cream, disliked taxes, loved animals, and cringed at the sight of spiders or slugs. Kristen was good, clean fun. She never made anyone feel belittled, awkward, or out of place.

If God makes himself visible in the lives of people, then he was visible in Kristen's. A glimpse of Kristen was a peek at the character of God.

When Kristen finished college she began working for a local youth center helping at-risk kids in the community. *At-risk* was the label they'd been given by society—a label given to any kid born within a nine-block radius of the community center. Anyone living in the apartment complexes in this area was exposed to violence, drugs, and sexual immorality every day. The average family survived on one welfare check and one parent (usually a mom) and an average of 3.6 kids.

Kristen worked in a youth center for the last four years. Each day the youth center attracted kids aged three to 18. Kristen loved them all as if they were her own. The center was 4,000 square feet in a strip mall next door to a liquor store. Old, torn carpeting covered the floors. The ceiling featured a pattern of broken and missing ceiling tiles. Hand-me-down couches surrounded an old console TV broadcasting more green than anything else. Old Formica counters and five or six dented metal stools—looking like donations from the local high school wood shop class—stood in one corner.

A rich church member on the upper west side of town funded the center, but volunteers were few and far between, so Kristen ran it mostly by herself. On any given day you'd find her behind the snack bar, on the old sectional couch surrounded by a pile of kids, or at the corner tables helping kids with their homework.

Everyone loved Kristen.

Kristen loved everyone.

But then she met Garth. No one liked Garth.

Garth was one of those kids who was really hard to love. When he walked into the youth center for the first time, Kristen heard an audible moan from all the other kids. They didn't even bother to whisper. They said, "What's *he* doing here?" and "There goes the youth center!"

Kristen quickly learned why.

Garth was loud and repulsive—even more than your average fifth-grader. It's hard to know where to begin to describe him. Apparently Garth didn't believe in bathing, and even if you somehow overlooked his greasy, unkempt hair, there's no way you could miss the putrid smell that floated around him wherever he went—a mix of dirty socks, locker-room stench...and onion ring belches.

His clothes caused some of the smell. They were filthy and worn. Garth always wore the same pair of pants, and usually his shirt was either one of only two T-shirts he owned, or a shoddy light blue button-up so dirty it looked like the car-repair guys in the auto shop across the street used it regularly as a rag.

To make matters worse, Garth always had a runny nose, and he apparently didn't know about the invention of Kleenex. He always had dried snot crusted around the bottom of his nose, across his upper lip, and trailing across the back of his hand where he always wiped it. Most of Garth's sentences ended with a deep snort, a second of silence, then a subtle chewing and swallowing.

The kids might've forgiven even this much—if not for his personality. Garth took things that didn't belong to him. He fought with others constantly. He never did his own homework, but he did make sure to disturb others to keep them from doing theirs.

Garth had no social skills. He was impossible to have a conversation with. He was insulting, laughing loudly and awkwardly at his own jokes—if you could call them jokes. "Eeeew! Kristen eats booger sandwiches!"

Kristen had her own battles with Garth. Every day he'd come in and ask for free food from the snack bar. Kristen was one of the most generous people alive. She always provided free snacks at activities and events. But the daily snack bar only featured snacks for sale, and these weren't movie theater prices, either. Seventy-five cents for a soda. Fifty cents for a candy bar. But every day Garth would beg, "Come on, Kristen, just hook me up with one candy bar. Who's gonna notice one candy bar?"

Kristen would kindly reply, "Garth, I can't give you special favors. You know everyone pays for candy."

Garth would sometimes become unruly. "What a rip! Can't even give away one candy bar. This place is sooooo lame!"

Kids usually came to Kristen's defense before she even had a chance to respond. They couldn't stand the sound of his whining.

No one liked Garth. Kristen even found *herself* wincing at the sound of his voice.

One March, Kristen took the center's elementary school kids on a field trip to the zoo. The school district provided buses, and local churches provided chaperones.

The trip went beautifully. The kids had a great time, no one got lost or injured, and by 5 p.m. the bus had dropped everyone off at the center.

Almost all the kids had left for home. Kristen stayed and chatted with the handful of students waiting for rides (because most walked home to the surrounding apartments). Finally the last student left with her ride.

Kristen locked up the center and was walking to her car when Garth walked out of the liquor store next door. He was looking down, drinking a soda, and hopping over lines on the sidewalk.

Instinctively, Kristen ducked her head and picked up the pace, hoping Garth wouldn't see her. He was at least 20 feet behind her. Maybe he wouldn't see.

"Kristen!"

No such luck.

She heard footsteps running up behind her. Kristen wished she could be anywhere else but on that sidewalk at that very moment. Before she even had a chance to turn around she felt his hand grab hers. "I'll walk with you," he said.

And he did, swinging Kristen's hand as they walked.

Kristen's first thought was, *Oh, no. This is the snotty hand—the one with the dried slime trail on it.* She literally cringed for a second.

She looked down at Garth's dirty little face. He smiled back up at her without even taking the straw from his mouth.

And that's when she heard it, almost audibly. She felt Jesus crying out, "Kristen, *it's me!*"

That morning Kristen had read a passage in Matthew where Jesus talked about how we treat others. He described how someday he would gather everyone together and hold them accountable for what they'd done. He would turn to a certain righteous person and thank him for feeding the hungry, giving the thirsty something to drink, inviting strangers in, clothing the naked, looking after the sick, and visiting those in prison.

The funny thing about this passage is that this righteous person doesn't even know about these acts of kindness. This person will ask Jesus, "When did we see you hungry and feed you, or thirsty and give you something to drink? When did we see you a stranger and invite you in, or needing clothes and clothe you? When did we see you sick or in prison and go to visit you?"

And Jesus will say, "I tell you the truth, whatever you did for one of the least of these brothers of mine, you did for me."

As Kristen looked down at Garth—dirty, stinky Garth—she heard Jesus. "*It's me!*"

At that moment she saw Garth differently. She actually held his crusty little hand just a little bit tighter, because she wasn't just showing kindness to a poor fifth-grader named Garth—she was showing kindness to Jesus.

TRANSITION STATEMENT:

All of us have Garths in our lives. Some might be the last people we'd ever want to reach out to—but they still need our love and kindness. Many of us might be having a drought of love right now, feeling as if we have nothing to give. That's why we need to connect to Christ. Jesus loves us despite our sinfulness and disobedience. As we feel that love, we can pass it on to others.

When Jesus walked this earth, he demonstrated love with his actions. He fed the poor, healed the sick, and showed love and compassion to the unloved and the undeserving.

When we do the same, we do it to Jesus.

APPLICATION AND SCRIPTURE:

Jesus tells us that someday he'll gather us together and hold us accountable for how we treated others. In Matthew 25 he describes what this will look like: "The King will reply, 'Truly I tell you, whatever you did for one of the least of these brothers and sisters of mine, you did for me.'" (Matthew 25:40)

CLOSING:

The Garths in our lives seem impossible to love. But with God's love in us, we can reach out to them.

I want you to close your eyes and think about yourself, and not those around you. Some of us might feel like Kristen felt with Garth. We might be having trouble loving someone near us. Listen, because right now you might hear Jesus telling you, "It's me. Whatever you do to this person, you do to me. However you treat this person, you treat me."

As you sit with your eyes closed and head bowed, maybe you need to make a decision to let Christ's love flow through you to others. If you have no love left to give, then accept Christ's love and forgiveness for yourself. As you allow yourself to be loved, you will overflow with love...even enough for the Garth in your life.

Let's pray right now.

TALK 03

TITLE: DO THE RIGHT THING

TOPIC: Integrity

BIG IDEA: We need to do what's right, not what's personally beneficial.

SCRIPTURE:

> "Lord, who may dwell in your sanctuary? Who may live on your holy hill? He whose walk is blameless and who does what is righteous, who speaks the truth from his heart and has no slander on his tongue, who does his neighbor no wrong and casts no slur on his fellow-man, who despises a vile man but honors those who fear the Lord, who keeps his oath even when it hurts."
> (Psalm 15:1-4, NIV)

PARTICULARS:

This true story is great for illustrating integrity. For most of you, this short talk will take a little less than 10 minutes.

THE STORY:

It seemed like any other day for Charles Moore, a 59-year-old Detroit homeless man. He started making his rounds of the streets early that day, digging through the garbage, looking for returnable bottles.

It's amazing what people throw away. Moore was barely able to scratch a living on what he collected from the garbage. Returnable bottles were the best commodity. A homeless person could collect enough returnable bottles in one day to earn food for three days.

On this particular day, Moore found a white envelope in the trash. Opening the envelope, he found $21,000 in U.S. savings bonds. Moore knew immediately what they were, because at one time he had owned bonds himself.

It was decision time. Keep the money...or do the right thing?

What would you do if you found that kind of money? What if you were homeless, out of work, and digging in garbage cans for recyclables as your main source of income? Would you keep the $21,000?

Think about it for a second: *What would you do?*

Moore was homeless, but he also had a moral compass that told him, "Somebody is missing these and would love to get them back." He said later that it didn't even enter his mind to keep the money for himself. "They weren't mine, and I knew that whoever they belonged to would miss them," he said.

But the owner didn't miss them. She didn't even know they were gone.

Fortunately for her, the right person found them—someone willing to do the right thing.

Moore immediately took the bonds to a local homeless shelter and turned them in. A staff member was able to find the owner of the bonds—a man who had died. His widow didn't even know the bonds existed. She'd never have known if Charles Moore hadn't returned them.

The bonds were returned to the widow. When she was told how they'd been returned, she tipped Moore $100.

One hundred dollars.

Thanks, lady!

Do you still think Moore did the right thing?

Moore was raised in the church in Ypsilanti, Michigan. Growing up, he was taught the difference between right and wrong. He had found himself homeless for the first time in his life after losing his job as a roofer.

Moore said, "My mother taught me to do the right thing. I was brought up in the church and I was just taught to do the right thing. The fact that the owners wouldn't have missed the bonds didn't make a difference to me. I know a lot of people say, 'I wouldn't have gave them bonds back, she didn't offer you but $100.' But I wasn't looking for $100. My purpose was to give them back to the rightful owner. That was the bottom line."

The reward didn't matter to Moore. He just wanted to do what was right.

The story doesn't end there.

When the story ran in Michigan papers, donations and support flooded in for Moore from people moved by his integrity. People gave him gifts of money, clothes, food, and even returnable bottles.

Dick Wolski, a Detroit man, helped pull together $1,200 for Moore: "What a lesson. Isn't that what we're all supposed to be doing?" he said.

Joseph Howse, a spokesperson for the Neighborhood Service Organization—the operators of the shelter Moore frequented—said, "Moore's actions should recast our ideas about the homeless. The next time you're walking down the street, that person you are brushing aside as *this homeless person* could someday be the person who gives you a helping hand. You just don't know who an angel is. That's why you help the least of these."

Where's Moore today? He now has an apartment and a car and is enrolled in a job-retraining program, learning computers. He hopes to own his own business one day.

But he didn't start his business with someone else's $21,000. Charles Moore was down and out, but he kept a strong sense of personal ethics and honesty that he didn't compromise even in a time of great personal need.

TRANSITION STATEMENT:

What would you have done?

Moore did the right thing with no expectation of reward. As it turned out, he got a fresh start because of his honesty.

But what if there had been no reward at all?

Is reward—or praise—the only reason to do right?

APPLICATION AND SCRIPTURE:

Let's face it—we face tough choices regularly. We might pray over these decisions and ask God's advice, because many decisions don't seem cut and dried: What college should I attend? What car should I buy? What job should I take? Sometimes we fret over decisions because both choices seem okay.

But there are decisions we don't have to pray about. We know what we should do because it's a choice between right and wrong.

But what good is it to just *know* what to do? Does morality stop at just knowing? It's one thing to know what to do; it's another thing to do it.

A young teacher wanted one particular job badly, but she didn't get the contract, so she signed a contract with another school district. A week later she was offered a job from the first district where she really wanted to work. She didn't know what to do, so she called her dad for advice. After listening to her ethical dilemma, he said to her, "Let me get this straight. You've signed a contract with one school district. Is that right?"

She said, "Yes, I have."

He replied, "I don't understand why we're having this conversation."

The Bible talks about this in Psalm 15:1-4.

In this Psalm, David speaks to us who may live in God's sanctuary, listing the traits of true followers of God:

Those whose walk is blameless, who do what is righteous, who speak the truth from their hearts...

Pay special attention to what David says in verse 4:

...who keep their oaths even when it hurts...

David describes followers of God as people who aren't honest only when it's convenient—they keep their word even when it hurts. They show integrity even when it hurts to be honest.

When was the last time it hurt you to be honest? When was the last time it hurt to keep a commitment or do the right thing?

In our Christian walk, the Bible tells us a great deal about right and wrong. Just as a good airline pilot must have a healthy fear of gravity and trust in the cockpit gauges, the Christian must have a healthy fear and respect for the Word of God. Making ethical decisions without the guidance of Scripture is foolish, even when it seems to cost us to follow what the Bible says.

CLOSING:

I'm going to pray. Let's take a minute and close our eyes and look totally at ourselves. Make a commitment right now to do right—even if it hurts.

Let's pray.

Source: *Detroit News*, July 22, 2006

TALK 04
TITLE: SAVE ME!

TOPIC: God Works in Hidden Ways

BIG IDEA: In the middle of all the bad things happening in our world, God is working for good behind the scenes.

SCRIPTURE:

> "And we know that in all things God works for the good of those who love him, who have been called according to his purpose." (Romans 8:28)

PARTICULARS:

I got the idea for this fictional story from my friend Mike over at MikeysFunnies.com (a daily email of good, clean humor). It gives kids a clear picture of how God can use bad circumstances for good. You can tell it in either 10 or 20 minutes, depending on how detailed you want to be.

THE STORY:

Brian had never paid much attention when flight attendants gave the safety instructions. He traveled to Malaysia once a month for business, so this 19-hour flight was as routine as ever—until now.

The oxygen masks dropped from above. Brian struggled to get the little elastic strap over his head and then helped the elderly lady sitting next to him. Screaming and wailing filled the cabin while stewardesses frantically ran from person to person yelling instructions and forcing a few people to sit down, put on their seat belts, and get into crash position.

Brian never felt the impact with the ocean. The captain guided the plane down as gently as he could, but the plane's impact with the water tore the fuselage in two. Brian remembered the flash of a huge flame and the feeling of cold water on his legs. And then... blackness.

When Brian woke up, he felt like he had knives in his throat. He coughed, wincing at the pain. It took him a few seconds to realize he was wet. As he wiggled his fingers, he felt sand. Before he opened his eyes he heard waves crashing and felt water flow up around his body. Salt water poured over his face and into his mouth.

Awake now, Brian jerked his body up and coughed, cringing again at the pain in his throat. The intense sun only allowed him to squint as he tried to adjust his eyes to the brightness.

Looking down, Brian saw white sand, small rocks, and thousands of tiny shells. He had never seen so many shells. He peered beyond the beach to the trees, but suddenly his stomach lurched and he hunched over and retched in the sand.

He sat for a moment, trying to remember where he was or where he'd been. The details were fuzzy. He remembered people panicking, screaming, a flash of light. He even remembered seeing the look on a woman's face across the aisle while he was bent over in crash position. Her eyes were wide open, unblinking, and tearing up. She never uttered a sound, but her face begged for help. It was the last clear moment Brian remembered.

Dazed, he sat there until his pants dried. The tide went out and the sun dried him as well as the sand around him.

Brian noticed he only had one shoe on. The left foot was bare and his pant leg was torn open near the bottom. He reached to investigate the pant leg, but stopped mid-reach when he realized his shoulder was hurt. This was when Brian discovered he wasn't wearing a shirt. He massaged his shoulder. It was sore and hard to move, but he was okay.

Brian struggled to his feet and looked up and down the beach, hoping to see something.

He saw nothing.

He looked toward the thick canopy of trees up the beach again. He walked to the trees and peeked inside. Insects and birds chattered and chirped overhead. There wasn't much to see, so Brian decided to explore the beach.

He picked up two logs and laid them down in a letter X on the beach, far out of the tide's reach, and circled the X by shuffling around it in the sand. He left his one shoe in the middle of the X and began walking east along the beach—or so he figured. If it was evening, he was traveling east, because his shadow stretched out in front of him.

Brian was still a little delirious. He couldn't seem to think much beyond *walk* and *look for any sign of life*. And that's when he finally thought to pray.

As he walked along the beach, one heavy step at a time, Brian cried out to God. He bypassed any greetings or thank-yous and got straight to business. "Please help me! Please help me!" He actually repeated the words aloud for a few miles—"Please help me."

After what seemed like hours, Brian stopped and stared at the length of beach ahead of him. He could only see about a mile in front of him before the beach curved to the right and disappeared. He turned and looked behind him. It was the same. He could see a mile, maybe two, before the beach disappeared to the left. Maybe he was on a peninsula and eventually he'd come to the mainland.

But as Brian walked, he only saw ocean beyond the curve. No land ever appeared in the distance.

Before long he noticed that he didn't see his shadow anymore. It was now right below him. The sun was getting higher. It wasn't evening. It had been morning when he left on his little walk, and now it was stretching into afternoon.

As hours passed, Brian began to doubt the logic of his little exploration. He remembered hearing people say things like, "Never leave your original location. Stay put and wait for someone to rescue you." Brian debated himself as he walked toward the sun.

When I left, he thought, *the sun was behind me. But then it was on top of me and to my right. Now it's in front of me again.*

He couldn't figure out how the sun had gotten in front of him. Was he going in circles? As he considered turning around, he noticed something in the distance.

Something was on the beach.

He stopped for a second and stared. The object wasn't moving.

Brian's walk gained a bounce as he approached the object. He wasn't sure what it was, but he'd seen nothing but beach for the entire day. Anything was better than that. He found himself almost jogging as he got closer to the dark object.

But about 50 yards away from the object, he came to a stop. His head dropped in disappointment. His shoulders sank as he realized what this meant. The object ahead of him was his shoe, sitting on top of two logs in the shape of a letter X.

Brian had gone in a complete circle.

He was on an island, and no other land was in sight. And he'd just seen every inch of beach on this entire island without one glimpse of anything other than sand and shells.

Brian collapsed into the sand and wept.

A few hours later, he awoke to the sensation of wetness again, but this time it wasn't from the ocean. It was rain.

In the glow of the setting sun, Brian ran around the beach with his mouth open, trying to catch raindrops in his mouth. After a few pointless minutes of this, he tore a large leaf off a tree and ran back to the beach. He cupped it as it filled with water, then dumped the water in his mouth. For the next hour, this routine occupied his time.

Later that night Brian leaned against a tree, staring into the sky. "God, please help me. Please send someone to save me."

It was a long night.

Two days later Brian sat in the shade of the beachside trees admiring his work. He had taken logs and large branches and written the word *HELP* 20 yards high by 50 yards long. Any passing plane could see it.

But as he sat admiring his work, his stomach grumbled.

Brian knew of one food source he'd declined several times already. But his hunger was turning to pain, and by this point, even the most disgusting food would be an improvement over the pain in his stomach. So Brian worked his way to a large fallen tree with peeling bark. He peeled it back and watched various insects scurry around the freshly exposed surface. Within seconds they disappeared. Brian pulled another piece of bark off. The same. Bugs scurried in every direction.

Five pieces of bark later, Brian had the courage to grab some bugs and shove them in his mouth. On the first attempt Brian realized it was better to smash them and kill them before eating them. It was no fun trying to swallow something crawling around inside his mouth.

After Brian finished dinner, he walked down to the shore again and looked for any sign of rescue. His prayers began to change from "Help me, Lord" to "Why me, Lord? Why me?"

Brian started fires each night. Fires were easy to start. He pulled his shoelace across a stick like a bow and spun another stick over some bark surrounded by dry grass. He had never been in the Boy Scouts, but it was amazing what he'd learned from watching enough special ops films.

Although there were many trees, fallen wood was scarce. So Brian kept his fires to a minimum most nights, wanting to save the wood for the coldest nights.

It rained again on the fourth night and Brian sat shivering next to a tree, soaked to the core. His fire sputtered out in minutes, and his source of warmth was gone. Brian decided he needed a shelter.

The next day Brian started constructing a shelter. He found several perfectly sized logs and started on the frame of his little hut. It took several days just to carve the notches in the wood so the frame would fit to Brian's liking. In the days that followed, Brian worked on branches for siding.

But it took him almost a week to figure out the exact design for his roof. He tried several combinations of branches but found them completely useless in blocking out the rain. He eventually discovered a way to braid leaves together and form a thicker ribbon to lay across the beams. He also found some long dry grass that—when woven together—made a canopy of sorts.

It took Brian almost four weeks to finish his shelter. Each night, his prayers grew shorter and bitterer.

The night he completed his shelter, he sat by the fire and looked up at the stars. He prayed the most sincere prayer he'd ever prayed in his life, crying out to God for help. He pleaded, "God, please! You know I've served you. You know I've made you number one in my life. God, I put my faith in you. I trust you!"

Brian realized he'd been grumbling quite a bit on the island. Part of him thought, "Well, who wouldn't complain if *this* happened to him?" But in his heart, he felt that if he truly trusted God, he would trust him even in this.

Brian swallowed hard and looked up to the skies again. "God, I trust you. Please save me from this. Please save me."

He fell asleep on the beach under the stars.

In the morning, Brian awoke to a cold breeze. The coals from last night's fire glowed when the wind blew, so Brian grabbed some dry grass and started his fire again.

When his stomach growled, he thought about trying his hand at spearfishing. The thought of fish roasting over a fire gave him renewed energy. He grabbed a sharpened stick and went down to the ocean.

Brian fished for hours with no luck. Discouraged and frustrated, ready to give up, he decided to go back up the beach. He heard a crackling sound from the beach and turned to see his little hut engulfed in flames. The wind had carried some debris from his fire to the hut.

Brian had built his fire a good 20 yards from the hut because he knew the danger of his hut catching fire. But he hadn't considered the wind.

He sprinted to the hut and threw sand at the fire, but after a dozen futile handfuls, he fell back in exhaustion and witnessed almost a month's worth of work go up in flames. He wept as flames shot 20 feet into the air.

At the end of his rope, Brian cursed God. "Why have you done this to me? Didn't you hear my prayer? I cried out to you and you don't even listen. I ask you for help, and you bring me *this*!"

He rolled over and cried into the sand. Finally, exhausted, he fell asleep mumbling, "Why me? Why? Why?"

Brian dreamed of being home. He dreamed of pulling out of his driveway in his Nissan Pathfinder, listening to the radio, and sipping on coffee. He drove down his street waving to his neighbors — but then his dream took a turn for the worse. A huge horn blared as a semi truck drove right at him! It blared its horn again. The noise was so loud it woke him up. He sat bolt upright in the sand.

The horn sounded again. It echoed across the beach.

It took Brian a few seconds to realize that he was awake.

The horn sounded yet again.

Brian turned around and looked past the burning ashes of his hut. A huge ship sat a few hundred yards from the beach, and a small boat with three men was approaching the beach.

Two hours later Brian sat on the deck of a huge oil rig, wrapped in blankets and sipping hot coffee.

"How'd you ever find me?" Brian asked.

"We saw your signal fire," they replied.

TRANSITION STATEMENT:

"God. I trust you. Please save me from this. Please save me."

Those were Brian's words. God heard his cry and helped him by making a 20-foot signal fire out of Brian's hut at the exact right moment.

But Brian didn't know that.

God works in ways we don't even see. We have no idea why God does the things he does. What we do know is that God loves us all so much he has given everyone free will. Because of this, the world is a sinful, sometimes evil place.

Yet in the middle of all the bad things that happen, God is there for us.

Sometimes we just don't see it.

APPLICATION AND SCRIPTURE:

Don't you get annoyed when you're in pain and a Christian friend pulls out Romans 8:28: "And we know that in all things God works for the good of those who love him, who have been called according to his purpose." You want to yell,

> Good????

> There's nothing good now—and there'll never *be* anything good—about what I'm going through.

> And all for God's purpose?

The most irritating thing when most people quote that verse is that they don't realize that when Paul wrote it, he was actually feeling pretty good. Paul was staying in the home of his good friend, Gaius, in Corinth (Romans 16:23). And this home was no small house—it was big enough to host all the churches of Corinth when they decided to meet together. Not too shabby. And Paul was writing to a thriving Roman church started mostly by people from all over Greece whom Paul himself had led to Christ (Romans 16).

Paul probably couldn't help but be pumped that his ministry had reached the great city of Rome. He was feeling great. And he was planning a new trip, always an exciting thing to do. His trip would take him to Jerusalem, Rome, and finally to Spain. Paul was a visionary with huge goals (Romans 15:14-33). In this pumped-up frame of mind, Paul wrote the verse you just heard.

That famous verse Paul wrote in Gaius' home would become prophetic:

> He was arrested in Jerusalem and shipped off to Rome—not exactly the way he had planned. How was this good?

> He appeared in chains as a prisoner—not exactly the way he

planned to appear before the kings. How was this good?

> He ended up in prison—not exactly the way he planned. How was this good?

But while in prison in Rome, he became a famous, best-selling author. Ever read the books of Galatians, Ephesians, Philippians, Colossians, and Philemon? They're some of the most-read books of the biggest best-seller—the Bible.

I don't know if Paul knew while in prison what kind of impact his writings would eventually have—but just as Brian didn't know what God was doing when his shelter burned to the ground, God had something even bigger in mind for Paul.

CLOSING:

So if you're in pain today, I don't want to just quote you Romans 8:28. But if you look at it on your own, I think you'll find comfort in the fulfillment of that verse in Paul's life. In addition, read the book of Philippians—a book of how you can rejoice in everything God is doing even though you can't always see what that is. And while you're reading, remember that Paul wrote Philippians while chained in a Roman prison, awaiting his execution.

Sample Prayer: *Father God, your Word is a comfort to me. Help me remember the story of Brian and the story of Paul, who couldn't see what you were doing but trusted you anyway. And help me to trust you to work out that good from my pain.*

TALK 05

TITLE: SEMI ANGRY

TOPIC: Anger

BIG IDEA: Jesus can free us from the world of selfishness and bitterness.

SCRIPTURE:

> "But the Lord replied, 'Is it right for you to be angry?'" (Jonah 4:4)

PARTICULARS:

This true story is about the power of anger. As you wrap up this talk, focus on the root of anger and communicate the fact that anger in and of itself is not wrong.

THE STORY:

When Michael Eck looked into the rearview mirror, all he could see was the grille of a semi.

Michael's car was hit so hard his engine died. On a Chevy Impala, that meant no power steering, no power brakes—no power, period. This wouldn't have been so bad if Michael had been able to pull over. But the semi downshifted and came at him again, pushing Michael's car down the freeway like a toy car.

He was trapped. He thought he was going to die.

So how did Michael, a former truck driver himself, get himself in a road rage scrap with the driver of a massive Peterbilt 18-wheeler?

On this day, Michael left for work in the afternoon, allowing plenty of time to get to his job as a forklift operator. The road was I-83 in Pennsylvania, the same road he'd taken to work for 12 years.

Before the forklift, Michael drove trucks across the U.S., so he sympathized with the truckers on I-83, a narrow road with small shoulders. If vehicles stalled or got in an accident, there was little room for trucks to pass.

At 2:50 p.m. Michael and several other cars caught up with a blue 18-wheeler hauling two earthmovers. The vehicles were approaching an incline, so Michael decided to pass the truck to avoid getting stuck behind it, as anyone would have. Michael signaled, passed the truck, and returned to the left-hand lane.

As Michael climbed the hill, he caught up with slower traffic and tapped his brakes.

That's when the first impact occurred.

Michael felt a light tap, the kind that barely dents a bumper. When he glanced in his rearview mirror, he saw the grille of the large blue Peterbilt he'd just passed.

Michael knew they needed to pull over, check for damage, and exchange insurance information. But he looked at the time and realized he really didn't need this right now. He'd left his house early enough, but following up this accident could make him late for work.

Michael didn't want to pull onto the narrow shoulder, so he looked to the right-hand lane to see if he and the truck driver could merge into that lane. Traffic was thick—it was going to be hard to get over.

But something else was wrong.

The truck wasn't even trying to merge. Before Michael had a chance to put two and two together, he heard the truck downshift and saw it surge toward him again.

WHAM!

The truck hit Michael so hard it snapped him back in his seat. Michael's engine died and he lost all power.

For the first time Michael thought, *This guy's intentionally ramming me.*

The truck shifted gears again and smacked into Michael's car, this time pushing it up I-83 with traffic. Michael tried to steer, but it was difficult. With no power, the car was almost impossible to control.

Michael quickly punched in 911 on his cell phone and returned his hands to the wheel. Fortunately, he had a hands-free setup in his car and could talk using the microphone in his visor.

"I just got rear-ended three times by a Peterbilt on I-83. Can you help me?"

The dispatcher asked Michael questions about his location. Michael gave him what he knew and asked him to hurry. "I'm being pushed, literally," he added.

Trooper Serell Ulrich was on duty at the station when the call came. He rushed to his car and got on I-83 in minutes, but he saw a traffic jam of rubberneckers observing the truck-car collision. Ulrich estimated he was 10 minutes from Michael's location.

Meanwhile, Michael was still being pushed up the freeway like a child's toy in the hands of a bully. "Where's that officer?" he pleaded into the phone.

His speedometer died when he lost power, but Michael figured they were moving at 40 to 50 miles per hour.

Michael watched the right-hand lane, looking for an opening, but traffic was so thick it was almost impossible to find one—especially with no power.

Finally, Michael saw daylight. He steered as hard as he could and rolled into the other lane. But the truck followed and slammed into him again, continuing to push him up the road. Michael had no idea how long his Impala could take this kind of abuse. He was sure this wasn't going to end well.

Up the road, Ulrich reached a place where he could navigate to the shoulder. With only a few inches of clearance on each side, he drove north toward Michael's location.

Michael was in serious jeopardy at this point. The truck pushed him violently up I-83 as they approached another hill. Michael could see another huge truck moving slowly up the hill. The gap began to close. Michael's car was going to be smashed between the two trucks.

I'm going to die, he thought.

He looked for an escape. The lanes around him were full.

He was trapped.

Michael actually thought about opening his door and bailing out. He figured, *Sure, I'll hit the pavement at 40 miles an hour, and the truck will probably run me over. But at least it's a chance!*

Michael was about to reach for the door handle when flashing lights passed him on the right-hand side. A state trooper!

Trooper Ulrich had finally broken free of traffic and arrived in the nick of time. He flashed his lights at the cars to pull over. When the Peterbilt saw the trooper, he braked, letting the Impala coast to a stop on the shoulder.

Michael almost kissed the ground when he got out of his car.

The huge blue semi pulled over and stopped on the shoulder, its engine still running.

Who could possibly be inside?

What incredible sin had Michael committed to deserve this life-threatening assault?

As the trooper cautiously approached the Peterbilt, he saw the driver—a small, 65-year-old man hunched behind the wheel.

Trooper Ulrich demanded, "What's going on?"

The silver-haired driver, James Trimble, was shaking all over with boiling rage. In a hot surge of anger he yelled at the trooper, "This guy cut me off!"

Investigators determined that the 18-wheeler had smashed and pushed Michael for 12 miles up I-83. This outburst of uncontrolled road rage lasted more than 20 minutes. Trimble, who pleaded guilty to one count of aggravated assault and six lesser charges, agreed to undergo psychological evaluation and surrender his commercial driver's license—forever. He was sentenced to two years in prison.

Michael Eck quit his forklift job and now—of all jobs he could've chosen—drives 18-wheelers again.

TRANSITION STATEMENT:

What caused a slight, stooped, white-haired old man to morph into a mad, raging, wild beast?

What causes hot outbursts of anger and loss of self-control?

We all have hot buttons. Sometimes those hot buttons are other people—people who just make us mad. Sometimes those hot buttons are things that don't work—especially computers or automobiles. Sometimes those hot buttons are stupid drivers, or traffic conditions.

These things are the cause of our anger—or are they?

Are circumstances really the cause of our anger? If that's true, why do we sometimes get angry for little or no reason? Let's be honest. Haven't you ever just had a really bad day—a day where even the smallest thing sets you off?

Now think about the opposite kind of day—maybe a day when you heard some really good news. Do you notice it's *hard* to get angry during this kind of day? Someone could do something really bad, but we're more likely to just let it go on such a good day.

Why?

Because of the world our minds choose to live in.

APPLICATION AND SCRIPTURE:

Some of us choose to live in a volcano of selfishness. Bottom line: We're self-seeking. And when something gets in the way of *our* way, we explode. We walk around ready to explode at any moment.

Such was the plight of the little old man in this story. He was living in a world of selfishness and bitterness.

We need to get out of that world.

In the Bible we can read about a guy just like this. His name was Jonah. Sure, some of you might remember the account of Jonah and the big fish. But do you remember the world he chose to live in? This guy lived in a world of hate. He hated the people of Nineveh, and because of it, he got angry at everyone who crossed his path. When God had compassion on Nineveh, Jonah got angry. Think of that: Jonah got angry because God was merciful.

That might sound harsh, but that's what Jonah was like. When God had compassion on Nineveh, Jonah exploded. He wanted them all to get hit by a bus. Jonah was an angry person—that's why he ran from God and got swallowed by the big fish in the first place. He even got mad at a worm. Jonah had some serious issues.

Why?

Because of the world he chose to live in.

He chose to live in a world of selfishness, hate, and bitterness. It didn't matter what happened to him—he was destined to explode.

Some of us are living in that world, too.

The trucker in this story was living in that world. And look where it got him.

When Jonah lived in that world, God asked him, "Is it right for you to be angry?" (Jonah 4:4, 9) The answer is no. And most of us sitting here already know that living in the volcano of selfishness and bitterness isn't right.

We need to get out of that world.

CLOSING:

I want you to close your eyes and think about yourself, not those around you. I'm going to pray, but before I do, let me ask you: What world are you living in? Are you living in a volcano of selfishness and bitterness, ready to explode at the slightest thing? As crazy as it sounds, could that be you driving that semi someday?

What world are you living in?

It's not about anger management; it's not about counting to 10. Some of us just need to leave that world of selfishness. Jesus can free you from that world. If you're willing to put your trust in him, Jesus will let you in his world. And his world is a world of love, hope, peace, and patience. When Jesus is in charge of your world, you can just kick back and let him drive. When he's in charge, you'll be free from the pressure of the world of anger and selfishness.

Let's pray.

Source: Based on a story from *Reader's Digest*, Malcom McConnell, September 2001, at http://www.rd.com/content/openContent.do?contentId=26725

TALK 06
TITLE: WITH KIERRA

TOPIC: Lifestyle Evangelism

BIG IDEA: Our actions are our legacies.

SCRIPTURE:

> "In the same way, let your light shine before others, that they may see your good deeds and glorify your Father in heaven." (Matthew 5:16)

PARTICULARS:

This fictional story is based on the life of a girl from San Jose, California. Those who knew her believed they'd seen a true glimpse of what Christ is like.

THE STORY:

Just 16 when she was killed, Kierra's legacy lives on.

Kierra had just dropped off her friend Rebecca after soccer practice when—half a mile from her home—a drunk driver slammed into her gray Honda Civic, killing her instantly.

A week later, friends and family packed the 1,200-seat auditorium of a local church to honor a young girl—a walking, breathing glimpse of Jesus Christ.

Kierra was born into a household that didn't attend church. But that changed when she was four years old. Her father decided to visit the new neighborhood church on Easter Sunday, so the family dressed up in their best clothes. Kierra and her little sister wore Easter hats and little white dresses trimmed in lace.

Kierra's father stood up at the end of the service that day and made a commitment to follow Christ for the rest of his days. Apparently he meant it, because their family began attending church regularly, getting involved in many of the activities, and contributing generously to the church budget.

So Kierra grew up reading the Bible. The family started with Genesis and Exodus, jumped immediately to the Gospels, and then bounced around between the Old and the New Testaments.

At the age of seven, Kierra decided she wanted to begin her own relationship with Jesus. She prayed with her father in their living room, asking Jesus to be in charge of her life. She wrote that date in her Bible, and from that day on she enjoyed a growing relationship with God.

Kierra attended public schools. By middle school she was discouraged with what she saw around her. Her heart broke for her non-Christian friends. Not only were many of them hurting from the choices they made every day, they had no purpose in life. They seemed so empty.

At church, the youth leader taught youth group members how to share their faith. This thought terrified Kierra. She wanted to share with her friends, but she struggled with the actual words to say. It wasn't that she was scared of sharing Jesus if her friends asked her—she actually was rather articulate at explaining how to have a relationship with Christ. Her struggle was *how* to get to that point in the conversation. Her friends never actually asked her, "Can you tell me about Jesus?" And Kierra was a little apprehensive about bringing it up.

When Kierra was in ninth grade she was invited to a Young Life event at her school. Kierra had no idea what Young Life was, but the organization was throwing a huge Thanksgiving party and it sounded like fun, so she decided to attend. She quickly discovered that Young Life is a Christian organization. She developed a friendship with a staff member named DeAnna and started attending weekly meetings.

One week she and DeAnna talked about evangelism. Kierra shared her struggle with DeAnna. "I would love to tell my friends about a relationship with Jesus," she said, "but it's hard to know just how to start that conversation."

DeAnna understood and suggested something Kierra immediately took to heart. "Why don't you invite them to something where they'll hear about Jesus? Then you might be able to talk with them about it."

Kierra thought that was a great idea, and she began to invite her friends to Young Life events. By the end of the year, five of her unchurched friends regularly attended these events with her. All five loved Young Life, and they were attentive when DeAnna and other staff members led discussions. These discussions usually led to conversations about Jesus.

On the way home from these events Kierra often found opportunities to continue these conversations or ask her friends, "What did you think about that discussion?" She was never pushy or judgmental. Her friends saw her as a person they could talk openly with.

That summer, all five of Kierra's friends went to the weeklong Young Life Camp with her. The speaker clearly outlined what a relationship with Christ was all about. That summer two of Kierra's friends, Ashley and Alyssa, gave their lives to Christ and started attending church with her.

During Kierra's sophomore year, the six girls continued to hang out together. Kierra, Ashley, and Alyssa attended a Bible study, but all six attended Young Life midweek.

One of the six was Rebecca. Rebecca was the rebel in the bunch. She often found herself in trouble at school. It wasn't uncommon for her to fight and get suspended, and she knew the detention room well.

Kierra and Rebecca played soccer and carpooled home together every day. Kierra often invited Rebecca to hang out with the group on weekends, but sometimes Rebecca had other plans. Many of these plans involved partying or hooking up with the various boyfriends she kept, but Kierra never stopped inviting Rebecca or loving her for who she was. She just hugged Becky and told her, "You're always my Becky Bec!"

Kierra and the five girls went to camp again the summer before her junior year, where two more friends made a commitment to Jesus. Rebecca wasn't one of them. During most of Kierra's junior year, five of the six girls now attended the weekly Bible study at the church, and Rebecca slowly became the outcast of the group.

When Kierra turned 16 she got a car. She drove it to school every day. Since she and Rebecca were the only two in the group who played soccer, they drove home together every day. On Fridays, Rebecca often shared her weekend plans with Kierra.

If her plans didn't work out, Rebecca texted Kierra, "Where R U? Can I come over?"

Kierra always texted back, "Of course my Becky Bec!"

Rebecca often ended up crashing at Kierra's house for the weekend. Kierra was glad, because when Rebecca was there, she wasn't somewhere else getting in trouble.

One Wednesday night after soccer practice Kierra and Rebecca stopped at Dairy Queen on the way home. "My treat," said Kierra. Rebecca grabbed a corner table while Kierra ordered.

When Kierra flopped down across from Rebecca, she noticed Rebecca's eyes were teary. Kierra slid an Oreo Blizzard across the table and smiled, gathering her thoughts. "What's up, Bec?"

Rebecca didn't say anything. She just stirred her Blizzard slowly with a plastic spoon and let the tears pour down her face and drip onto the table.

Kierra considered probing some more, but she knew Rebecca

would talk when she was ready. They ate their Blizzards in silence. Kierra smiled at Rebecca and threw a napkin at her. Rebecca flicked some Oreo on Kierra's sweatshirt and managed a laugh.

On the way across the parking lot Kierra threw her left arm around Rebecca. "You talk to me if you need to, okay?"

Rebecca smiled and threw an arm around Kierra. They walked arm in arm to the car. "You know I will," she answered.

"You're always my Becky Bec!" Kierra said.

The next week Kierra was killed after dropping off Rebecca.

At the funeral, five girls gave speeches about a girl named Kierra who had changed their lives. Rebecca was last to speak.

Rebecca took a minute to gather her composure as she stood in front of the microphone. She looked out across the masses of people who had come to pay tribute to her friend. She hadn't prepared, and she didn't really know where to begin.

She eventually shared about a friend who loved her for who she was and in spite of all the things she was not. She shared stories of camp experiences and memorable trips home from soccer practice. Then she paused for what seemed like a solid minute. Looking down at the other four girls in the front row, Rebecca said, "There's one thing all five of us who spoke today have in common. All of us were pretty messed up three years ago." She wiped a tear with the back of her hand and laughed, "Some of us still are."

Everyone in the audience smiled. A few chuckled, a nice break from the cloud of anguish enveloping the room.

Rebecca continued, "But Kierra befriended us. She cared about us. And one by one, the five of us have come to our senses—all but one." Rebecca wiped away a tear with her wrist. "I've never quite taken that step. And I'll be honest with you, I don't know if I'm ready to."

The room was completely silent.

Rebecca continued, "But there's one thing I can say that my four friends in the front row would agree with wholeheartedly."

Rebecca's gaze panned the crowd, and she finished with these simple words:

"It was always easier to be good with Kierra around."

TRANSITION STATEMENT:

What an incredible legacy.

A 16-year-old girl not only reached out to her friends and introduced four of them to a relationship with Christ—she left an impression on both believers and unbelievers. "It was always easier to be good with Kierra around."

Wouldn't you like to leave a legacy like that?

"It was always easier to be good with Blake around." "It was always easier to be good with Ariel around." "It was always easier to be good with Josh around."

APPLICATION AND SCRIPTURE:

It's funny, but most of the time when the Bible talks about sharing our faith, it talks about our actions, not our words. Our actions are our legacies.

In the book of Matthew, chapter 5, Jesus gives a talk about being light in an amazing passage about affecting others eternally. He concludes with these words:

> "In the same way, let your light shine before others, that they may see your good deeds and glorify your Father in heaven." (Matthew 5:16)

Notice he doesn't say, "When they hear your good *words*..." He says, "When they see your good *deeds*..."

This isn't to say we aren't supposed to talk about Jesus. Even Kierra, who was terrified of talking about Jesus, talked with her friends about him.

But let's be honest. Talk is cheap. Many of us might say we follow Christ, but what do our actions say?

Our actions leave a legacy of who we are. A girl named Kierra left the legacy of an authentic follower of Christ. Her friends testified, "It was always easier to be good with Kierra around."

What a powerful legacy.

CLOSING:

As we close in prayer right now, I challenge you to think about the legacy you're leaving. What would people say at your funeral? What legacy are your actions leaving? Many of us might need to make a change right now.

Let's pray.

TALK 07

TITLE: UNRESTRAINED FRIENDSHIP

TOPIC: Christ, Our Friend

BIG IDEA: Unrestrained friendship might look weird to others—but who cares, when you care?

SCRIPTURE:

> "Six days before the Passover, Jesus came to Bethany, where Lazarus lived, whom Jesus had raised from the dead. Here a dinner was given in Jesus' honor. Martha served, while Lazarus was among those reclining at the table with him. Then Mary took about a pint of pure nard, an expensive perfume; she poured it on Jesus' feet and wiped his feet with her hair. And the house was filled with the fragrance of the perfume." (John 12:1-3)

PARTICULARS:

You may have heard stories like this before, but the following adaptation is based on a real-life example from a teacher. I was moved by the story and I've used it in school assemblies ever since.

THE STORY:

Nick was having a great year. For a shy, reserved sophomore who barely made the JV football team, that was a big deal.

Nick wasn't big—he was tall and lanky. But he could run the 40-yard dash faster than most, and he could catch anything thrown within 10 feet of him.

During the previous year—Nick's freshman year—he'd been just another kid at school. He was never found with the popular crowd or the jocks, but he wasn't found with the unpopular kids, either. Nick just blended in.

It's not a bad thing to blend in. Sometimes no attention is better than bad attention.

But when Nick joined the football team his sophomore year, things began to change. Nick proved himself one of the better players on the JV team. Girls Nick didn't even know greeted him along with the other players in the hallway. Other football players invited him to party with them or just hang out on Friday and Saturday nights.

Nick had graduated from blending in to joining the popular crowd.

The summer between Nick's sophomore and junior years he put on weight—not fat, but muscle, combined with a two-inch growth spurt. He worked on his skills and excelled in summer football camp. To Nick's surprise, he made the varsity team.

Nick's social circle began to expand. Three other varsity players—seniors Alec and Craig, and Vincent, a junior—became Nick's best friends. The four of them were inseparable. Wherever one was, the other three were nearby.

Nick's junior season started strong. In the first five games he caught 11 passes and scored two touchdowns. Alec, Craig, and Vincent grabbed him after one of the touchdowns and lifted him up on their shoulders. Nick never forgot that feeling—hands reaching up to give him high-fives, voices roaring as the crowd cheered.

Nick was happy.

Life was good.

But it ended faster than it began.

Nick took a hard hit in the first quarter of his sixth game. Everyone flinched when the linebacker hit him, but the real concern grew when Nick didn't get up. He was rushed to the hospital where doctors discovered he'd ruptured his spleen.

But this wasn't the worst of it. The surgeons ran some tests after the surgery because Nick's spleen shouldn't have been that large.

The Wednesday after the game, Nick and his mom got the bad news. Nick had Hodgkin's lymphoma. Since this cancer was one of the first to be determined curable, the doctors wasted no time determining what areas of the body were affected. They isolated it and started Nick on a combination chemotherapy treatment immediately.

Over the next few months, Nick endured the grueling effects of both chemo and radiation. Nick's mom would take him to the hospital once a day, or just a handful of visits a month, depending on the current treatment. Most days following a treatment, Nick felt nauseated and couldn't even attend his classes.

Then there was the hair loss.

When Nick lost his hair, he dropped out of school. His mom supported Nick's decision as long as he homeschooled and kept up his grades.

The treatments also meant no more football. Having the disease was bad enough, but the treatments left Nick too weak to work out and definitely too weak to play in a game. This was the hardest part for Nick. He loved football, and he loved everything it had done for him.

Nick's rise to stardom at his school had taken a year. In less than a month his whole life changed. He went from star player to not even being on the team—from being one of the most popular kids at school to being an isolated homeschooled kid. Worst of all, Nick had no idea if he'd even live to graduate.

After Nick stopped attending school, his three buddies visited once a week. The time was awkward at first. They didn't know what to say, and Nick didn't know how to respond. Nick felt especially self-conscious when he lost his hair. But Craig, Vincent, and Alec wore hats, so Nick did the same.

Friday nights were the worst. The whole town went to the football game, but Nick didn't. He used the disease as an excuse, but the reality was that he didn't want anyone to see him.

Nick had lost 20 pounds. He wasn't big to begin with, so losing 20 pounds left him looking emaciated. He thought that pale, emaciated, and bald weren't a winning combination for good looks. Lymphoma was beating him physically, but it was beating him much worse mentally.

Nick kept up the treatments for an entire year. The hospital where Nick was treated was hours away, but they made the trip faithfully.

As the year passed, Nick's body weakened and his mental state became more volatile. He never showed this side of himself to his friends. He kept it bottled up, sometimes bursting into tears in his bedroom or exploding in a tantrum at his mom over something trivial.

The doctor visits continued with no good news—until a Thursday afternoon during Nick's senior year.

Nick went to his regular appointment with his specialist for some routine tests. The doctor came back in an hour later, scratching his head. He said, "The results seem to be messed up. I'm sorry, Nick, but we need to retest."

Nick didn't say anything. He mumbled something to himself and allowed the doctor to do his job.

An hour later the doctor came in looking as if he'd seen a ghost. He asked Nick and his mom to sit down, which was weird, because they were already sitting down.

The doctor took his seat and said two words. "It's gone."

Nick and his mom didn't even react. They just stared at the doctor as if expecting more. Finally Nick's mom broke the silence. "I'm sorry—what?"

"It's gone," the doctor repeated. "It just...isn't there anymore."

This seemed to spark a little curiosity from Nick because he sat up in his chair and leaned forward. "What's gone?" Nick thought he knew what the doctor was saying—but he wasn't sure and he didn't want to allow himself any false hope. He'd been through entirely too much disappointment to go out on a bogus limb of hope.

A quirky smile crept onto the doctor's face. "The cancer. It's gone." The doctor stroked his chin, then shrugged his shoulders. "I don't want to steer you wrong. We do have a high success rate with curing this. But based on your last visit—let's just say I've never seen it take a turn for the better this fast. But it's gone. I kid you not."

Nick and his mom looked at each other, still skeptical.

The doctor went on, sensing their skepticism. "I thought the same thing. But I checked and rechecked. We even used a different machine. I don't want to make a mistake on this kind of thing. But Nick, you're healed!" He pointed to the ceiling with his forefinger and raised his eyebrows. "You've got someone up there looking out for you."

Nick's mom burst into tears of joy and threw her arms around Nick.

Nick just sat there looking bewildered. He smiled for a few moments, but seemed lost in thought.

While the staff did paperwork, Nick's mom made a few calls.

Nick was silent as they rode home. He seemed lost in another world. To him, the long drive seemed like a trip through time.

Nick pulled down the passenger side mirror in the car and looked at himself. He had avoided looking in the mirror as much as possible in the last year because he didn't like what he saw.

But for some reason, sitting in that car, he wanted to see what he looked like. Something was bothering him and his mom sensed it. About halfway home she asked him. "Nick, baby. What's wrong? You just got the best news in the whole world."

Nick didn't say anything. He just stared out the window.

His mother reached over and put her hand on Nick's knee. "Nick?"

Nick looked at his mom with tears streaming down his face. "I'm happy, Mom. I really am. I just know that things are going to be different now."

His mom reached over and wiped a tear from his face, trying to not take her eyes off the road. "What do you mean, Nick?"

Nick thought for a moment. He grabbed a Kleenex from the glove compartment and blew his nose. "I guess I gave up hope. I figured I'd never have to enter that campus again. And I don't want to. Especially looking like..." Nick pulled the visor down and pointed to the mirror, "...that!"

Nick's mom looked at Nick again and placed her hand on his cheek. "Oh, Nick." She wanted to say more, but in a year with Nick she'd learned not to force conversation when Nick had nothing to say.

They pulled into the driveway and Nick slowly got out of the car.

His mom grabbed the small cooler out of the back seat, Nick grabbed a folder with some of the hospital paperwork, and the two of them walked to the front door. She unlocked the front door and slipped the key back into her purse. Nick was the first to walk in.

"Surprise!" shouted the voices of almost 60 football players. Nick's mom had no idea how they all fit in their small living room, but there they were, all wearing their football jerseys—all with freshly shaved heads.

Nick swallowed hard. He couldn't speak.

Three familiar but bald faces were on hand next to the entry-way. It was Alec, Vincent, and Craig. Craig had even shaved his shaggy little goatee—Nick couldn't help but think he looked a little bit stupid. But there they were, backed up by the entire team. Like a bunch of cue balls, sitting there shining in the cheap 60-watt lighting.

Alec spoke up. "We heard the good news, and we want you back at school. But we figured you might want to fit in with the rest of us." Alec rubbed his freshly shaved head and sprang up to hug Nick. This set in motion a rush of 60 bald football players rushing to hug Nick, demolishing two end tables and a coffee table in the process.

Nick returned to school the next day—because his friends did something simple and selfless, but gutsy. But that one choice, that one selfless act by Nick's friends, made a huge impact on Nick's life.

TRANSITION STATEMENT:

Nick's three friends demonstrated unrestrained friendship. They were willing to make fools of themselves because of their love for their friend. When three people were willing to make a friendship statement, 60 football players followed. Unrestrained friendship can look weird to others—but who cares, when you care?

Jesus called us his friends (John 15:13-14). We know what unrestrained friendship meant to Jesus—he died for us. That's the ultimate cost of friendship.

What have you done to demonstrate your unrestrained friendship with Christ?

APPLICATION AND SCRIPTURE:

John 12:1-3 tells a story about what it means to be a friend of Jesus. Mary, like Nick's friends, was willing to put aside what people thought about her and commit an outlandish, unrestrained act of love toward Jesus.

"Six days before the Passover, Jesus came to Bethany, where Lazarus lived, whom Jesus had raised from the dead. Here a dinner was given in Jesus' honor. Martha served, while Lazarus was among those reclining at the table with him. Then Mary took about a pint of pure nard, an expensive perfume; she poured it on Jesus' feet and wiped his feet with her hair. And the house was filled with the fragrance of the perfume."

In the first place, Mary wasn't a servant. This task was beneath her, but she saw a need and filled it. Washing feet is not one of our customs today, so we may miss the meaning in her act. Guests' feet were usually dirty after travel, so it was customary to remove one's sandals upon arrival and wait for a servant to wash one's feet. Mary's act would be like the CEO of a company cleaning the company bathrooms. Mary was not a servant, but she humbled herself to wash Christ's feet anyway.

Second, Mary's act was costly. In verse 5 we learn that the perfume was worth about a year's wages.

And third, Mary literally "let her hair down." She went against the customs of the day in an act of unrestrained devotion. She was criticized for this act of friendship.

This story carries two themes. One is the act of unrestrained love and friendship of Mary toward a friend, but there's also Mary's recognition of an *eternal* friendship. She was willing to be denounced for her worship of Christ, not only as his friend, but as his servant.

In your life, what does a no-holds-barred, unedited relationship with Jesus look like? What does being unrestrained in your love for Christ look like for you? How do you feel about being criticized for your faith? If you didn't restrain or edit yourself, what would change in your relationships with loved ones? With strangers? With those who do not yet believe?

CLOSING:

Having looked at the unrestrained friendship and love of Nick's friends and of Mary, let's pray for each other so we can find ways to show unrestrained devotion to God during this week.

Sample Prayer: *God, too often I'm concerned about what others think of my acts of friendship and love for Christ. I'm afraid to take a stand and lead others to take a stand. Help me be like Nick's friends and even more like Mary, who stood alone in her unrestrained love and acts of friendship toward Christ.*

TALK 08

TITLE: STEERING TOWARD DARKNESS

TOPIC: Sin

BIG IDEA: We don't notice our descent when we're in darkness.

SCRIPTURE:

> "For you were once darkness, but now you are light in the Lord. Live as children of light (for the fruit of the light consists in all goodness, righteousness and truth) and find out what pleases the Lord. Have nothing to do with the fruitless deeds of darkness, but rather expose them." (Ephesians 5:8-11)

PARTICULARS:

This is the true story of the crash of Flight 401 in December 1972. It's an amazing tale, and it always makes kids think.

THE STORY:

Four days after Christmas, families were traveling home from holiday visits with loved ones. Despite the busy season, Eastern Airlines Flight 401 had only 163 passengers and a crew of 13.

Only 73 of the 176 people on board would live to see the New Year.

Flight 401 left New York's John F. Kennedy Airport at 9:20 p.m. All was routine until the plane reached Miami International Airport at 11:32 p.m., and the copilot lowered the landing gear.

That's when it happened.

The little green light didn't go on.

The little green light is a simple indicator letting pilots know the landing gear is down. The fact that this light wasn't on can mean one of two things: Either the landing gear isn't down, or the little green light isn't working.

This usually wasn't a big deal. It had happened on other flights. Pilots routinely re-cycled the landing gear, giving it another try.

Still no green light.

The captain called the tower. They would delay the landing to figure out the problem. The tower instructed the plane to climb to 2,000 feet, and fly west over the Everglades.

Meanwhile, the crew removed the light assembly. The flight engineer climbed down to see if he could catch a glimpse of the landing gear. He hoped that by peering through the small viewing window in the avionics bay he'd be able to see whether the gear was down. If it was, they'd know it was just a bad light bulb and not a landing gear malfunction.

When the plane reached 2,000 feet, the copilot engaged the autopilot. About 80 seconds later the captain accidentally bumped the plane out of autopilot, much the same as a tap on the brakes bumps your car out of cruise control. It's possible the pilot accidentally switched modes while leaning against the steering column when he turned to talk to a crew member.

Regardless of how it happened, the autopilot switched to CWS mode—Control Wheel Steering. In this mode, small adjustments by the pilot are noted by the autopilot, altering the plane's course. Even a small tilt of the wheel is saved and executed by the autopilot. In this case, tiny forward pressure on the steering column caused the plane to start descending gradually into the dark Everglades.

The descent was so gradual that no one felt it. And because of the darkness, the pilot and copilot never realized they were descending.

The plane dropped hundreds of feet before a chime went off. The altitude-warning chime is located under the engineer's work station—but the engineer was below deck trying to see the landing gear. When investigators listened to the cockpit recording afterward, the pilot and copilot gave no indication of having heard the chime.

The plane was headed toward the ground, and no one knew it. After all, they were distracted by the urgent problem of this light bulb and failed to concentrate on what was truly important—flying the plane.

Eventually the copilot took the controls to start another turn.

At this point he noticed the discrepancy. The cockpit recordings reflect this:

Copilot: We did something to the altitude!

Pilot: What?

CP: We're still at 2,000—right?

P: Hey—what's happening here?

It was too late.

The plane was flying at 227 miles per hour when it hit the ground nearly 19 miles from the airport. When the main body of the plane hit, it slid through grass and water, disintegrating as it went. Ninety-four passengers and five crew members died instantly. When the plane finally came to a stop, 75 people had survived.

Two burned-out light bulbs—a $12 replacement expense—led to the tragic crash. When investigators examined the plane the next day, the landing gear was indeed in the down-and-locked position.

TRANSITION STATEMENT:

There is no autopilot in the Christian life.

Some of us think we can just go through life on autopilot. We don't even realize we're in danger. We don't even notice the warning signs.

Some of us have steered toward the darkness. I don't need to convince you or even explain to you what this darkness is. Many of us have allowed ourselves to grow comfortable keeping things in our lives that don't belong there—even though we know they aren't right. When it's dark, it's impossible to see the warning signs. In darkness, we don't even notice our descent. But it's happening, and it's only a matter of time before we crash.

APPLICATION AND SCRIPTURE:

In the book of Ephesians, Paul writes about the dangers of steering toward darkness. He wants us to wake up to the warning signs.

> "For you were once darkness, but now you are light in the Lord. Live as children of light (for the fruit of the light consists in all goodness, righteousness and truth) and find out what pleases the Lord. Have nothing to do with the fruitless deeds of darkness, but rather expose them." (Ephesians 5:8-11)

Notice that Paul doesn't say, "Be a little careful"—he says, *"Have nothing to do with* the fruitless deeds of darkness" (emphasis added).

CLOSING:

I want to end our time with prayer. I ask that you close your eyes and bow your heads for a moment so you can think about yourselves and not those around you. As some of us are sitting here in silence, we realize there's some stuff in our lives that doesn't belong there. We've steered toward the darkness, and we haven't even noticed our descent. But God sees this stuff, and we know we're heading toward disaster. Don't think you can leave your life on autopilot—the descent is gradual, but unavoidable. You need to deal with it now.

Let's pray.

Sources: http://www.freshgasflow.com/flight401.htm
http://eastern401.googlepages.com/

TALK 09

TITLE: JAKE'S LAST STAND

TOPIC: Lifestyle Evangelism

BIG IDEA: Words are cheap. Actions speak truth.

SCRIPTURE:

"But in your hearts revere Christ as Lord. Always be prepared to give an answer to everyone who asks you to give the reason for the hope that you have. But do this with gentleness and respect, keeping a clear conscience, so that those who speak maliciously against your good behavior in Christ may be ashamed of their slander." (1 Peter 3:15-16)

PARTICULARS:

I wrote this fictional story based on an experience I had in high school (as embarrassing as it is to admit). I love using this story when talking to kids about sharing their faith, because sharing our faith is so much more than the words we speak.

THE STORY:

To Jake, it seemed like any other school day.

Jake went to lunch, then biology. Biology was hard, but even worse, it was boring. Ms. Spencer was a living sleeping pill. Her monotone voice could get anyone snoozing in less than five minutes, but she expected the class to hang on every word she uttered as if it were doctrine.

On this particular Tuesday Jake dozed off in the second row, the same as any other day. But suddenly his ears perked up and his head came up. He looked at Ms. Spencer to make sure he was hearing correctly.

He was.

She was talking about the Big Bang as if it were a fact. According to Ms. Spencer, all life originated from this one big explosion.

Was this the time to speak up?

According to his Sunday school teacher, it was. This was the moment he'd been waiting for. He remembered Mark's words clearly: "When the school tries to tell you what to believe, always be prepared to give an answer for what you believe." Mark drilled it into their heads over and over again: "Always be prepared to give an answer for what you believe." Jake remembered it was a verse somewhere in 1 Peter.

And Jake *was* prepared. He and the rest of the Sunday school class had studied evolution and learned how to poke holes in the theory. Their Sunday school teacher made sure that they used the word *theory* when talking about evolution. That was one of his pet peeves—public-school teachers treating evolution as fact.

As Jake sat there listening, he tried to work up the courage to speak up. He waited for the right moment. *Always be prepared to give an answer for what you believe. Always be prepared to give an answer for what you believe. Always be prepared to give an answer...*

It was time.

Jake stood up.

"I don't believe any of this."

The other students stirred from their sleep. Eyes around the classroom began to open and heads to turn toward Jake. Even James awoke from his slumber in the back row, wiping the drool off his desk while trying to adjust his eyes to the bright lights of the classroom.

With a captive audience, Jake continued, "This is just a theory."

Ms. Spencer paused for a moment, contemplating her words carefully. "Yes, Jake, this is a theory. A scientific theory supported by evidence, and sustained by most of the brilliant scholars across the planet."

All eyes bounced back to Jake. Jake swallowed hard and began his rehearsed answer.

The argument lasted less than a minute. Jake said a few words, Ms. Spencer giggled and retorted, belittling him. Jake tried to offer another argument, and Ms. Spencer cut him off, ending the exchange by switching to another subject.

As Jake sat back down in his chair he thought to himself, *Blessed are those who are persecuted for their righteousness.*

But the story doesn't end there. It picks up at the same desk in the same classroom, exactly two weeks later.

Most of the students had forgotten about the little incident. Jake hadn't. He told his Sunday school teacher at church, and he congratulated Jake, adding a brief lecture on things Jake could've said to add to his argument.

But none of that mattered at the moment. The only thing that mattered was the incredibly difficult test in front of Jake right now.

Ms. Spencer had warned the students about this exam for weeks. As a matter of fact, she'd been reviewing that very material before the incident two weeks before. As far as Ms. Spencer was concerned, the class had had plenty of time to study.

The night before the test, after dinner, Jake decided he'd better study. So he went to his room, opened his book, and pulled out his biology notes. After about 30 minutes of highlighting important facts and reviewing key notes Ms. Spencer had emphasized, Jake felt overwhelmed. He had most of the data right there in front of him, but it was a lot to memorize.

Jake paused to contemplate the situation. He knew he had literally hours of studying to do to even pass this test. It was overwhelming. Jake never considered the fact that he should've been preparing for this exam for weeks.

Jake thought about his parents' lecture on grades. He usually got pretty good grades. The lowest he'd ever earned was a C, although he got a D on a progress report once. His dad made it abundantly clear that a D was unacceptable. Jake would be grounded from everything if he ever got a D—even the church's mission trip during spring break.

Jake loved his church's Mexico trip. The whole youth group went to an orphanage in Mexico during spring break each year to play with the children and do building projects. It was a blast. He always had a great time with his friends. The group spent two days on the beaches of San Diego on the way back. It was by far one of the highlights of his year.

But if Jake didn't do well enough on this test—no Mexico trip.

Jake felt crushed by the pressure. He looked at all the data in his notes. If only he could memorize everything.

He sat in silence. Any outside observer would've thought he was just spacing. But Jake was making a decision. He was justifying what he was about to do. The answer was clear. He was just trying to convince his conscience.

Bad grade on the test, no trip, he thought.

I know God wants me to go on this trip. So maybe cheating this once isn't so bad.

The next day Jake sat in his desk in the second row, using the person in front of him to block the little cheat sheet he'd made the night before. If the teacher came anywhere close to him, he'd slide the cheat sheet under the test and out of sight.

He was halfway through the test when it happened. He had no idea how she knew or how she saw—but she did.

Ms. Spencer walked right up to Jake's desk. He had the cheat sheet tucked neatly under the test, but Ms. Spencer reached down, grabbed his test, and lifted it, exposing Jake's cheat sheet.

Jake couldn't breathe. The next second seemed to take an hour. Ms. Spencer glared at him with what looked like an evil smirk on her face. The blood rushed to her face, making her blonde roots almost glow.

"Look what we have here," Ms. Spencer said, picking up Jake's cheat sheet and showing it to the classroom. "A custom-made little cheater's guide!"

Everyone else in the classroom popped their heads up from their own tests, many of them tucking their own cheat sheets deep into the sleeves of their shirts.

Jake couldn't talk. He stared down at his desk. Ms. Spencer only got louder.

"So, is this the kind of work we can expect from Jake? Maybe this is the kind of work he's been giving us all year." She glared at Jake, but he didn't even notice. He was slowly melting into his seat, trying desperately to disappear into thin air.

"Maybe we should assume that he's been cheating like this all year," she continued. "Maybe we need to just fail him since he's obviously been cheating like this all year!"

This got Jake's attention. He still didn't speak, but he shook his head "no" hastily.

Ms. Spencer darted to the front of the room behind her desk and picked up the class phone, calling the front office.

"Get me Mr. Sawyer."

A pause.

"Mr. Sawyer, this is Ms. Spencer. I'm sending you Jake Fox, whom I've just caught cheating on our midterm exam."

Pause.

"Yes, and since I can only assume that he's been doing this all year long…" another short pause…"I think he should fail this class!"

Jake shook his head "no" again, helplessly.

Ms. Spencer nodded "yes" back to Jake as she listened on the line.

Two minutes later, Jake was collecting all his stuff and heading to the office.

Funny thing: If you met any of Jake's classmates that year and asked them about Jake, not a single one of them could've told you one word of Jake's comments to Ms. Spencer about his beliefs. But not one classmate will *ever* forget the day Jake was caught cheating.

It's too bad, really. Jake's Sunday school teacher may have had good intentions when he emphasized to Jake and his friends over and over again, *"Always be prepared to give an answer for what you believe."*

Too bad he misquoted the Bible.

And too bad the whole Sunday school class, including Jake, missed what the Bible was saying.

TRANSITION STATEMENT:

Jake learned a hard lesson that year: Words are cheap. Actions speak truth.

No one remembers Jake's words. But they all remember his actions.

APPLICATION AND SCRIPTURE:

Jake had been led astray. Instead of being taught character, the power of a life of integrity—Jake had been taught to argue.

And Jake's Sunday school teacher not only misquoted 1 Peter 3:15, he missed what the verse is saying. The emphasis isn't "Always be prepared." The emphasis is making Christ the Lord of our lives so centrally that others *see* the hope in us.

It isn't about what we say—it's about what others *see* in us.

Listen to 1 Peter 3:15-16 for yourselves:

> "But in your hearts revere Christ as Lord. Always
> be prepared to give an answer to everyone who asks
> you to give the reason for the hope that you have.
> But do this with gentleness and respect, keeping a
> clear conscience, so that those who speak maliciously
> against your good behavior in Christ may be ashamed
> of their slander."

Guess what? No one's ever going to ask us to give a reason for the hope we have unless hope is seen in our lives.

And that's where Jake was led astray. That's where his Sunday school teacher was wrong. So many believers in Christ are taught *what to say,* but they aren't taught *how to live.* And frankly, many of us need to just shut our mouths and start living the life. Our friends can smell a fake a mile away.

When it comes to sharing our beliefs with others, one of the main passages people use is from Matthew 5, where Jesus tells the story of salt and light. Jesus wraps up that talk with verse 16:

> "In the same way, let your light shine before oth-
> ers, *that they may see your good deeds and glorify
> your Father in heaven.*" (emphasis mine)

Notice that the verse doesn't say, "...that they may hear our babbling." Just like the verse in 1 Peter, this verse talks about what others see in our lives.

One of the best ways Jake could've spoken loudly to his classroom was by living a life of integrity. Not by living a false front just to look good, but by being exactly who he said he was—a follower of Christ.

Very few people will remember our words. But they'll all remember our actions. Authentic lives will open the doors to authentic conversations.

CLOSING:

Our daily choices have a huge impact on those around us. The choice to cheat. The choice to gossip. The choice to drive recklessly. The choice to lie.

Our friends notice these seemingly small elements of our lives. One of the best ways we can let our light shine before others is by *living* in the light—not just talking about it.

TALK 10
TITLE: FREEDOM FROM HATE

TOPIC: Forgiveness

BIG IDEA: Forgiveness is the miracle of a new beginning.

SCRIPTURE:

> "Be kind and compassionate to one another, forgiving each other, just as in Christ God forgave you."
> (Ephesians 4:32)

PARTICULARS:

This is an inspiring (and true) story of the freedom that forgiveness provides.

THE STORY:

Your senior year of high school should be one of the best years of your life. But Greg Wittkamper's senior year was the worst of his life.

It started at the beginning of the school year, 1965. Greg,

who's white, went to school with four black students at Americus High School in Georgia—and a mob pelted his car with rocks and bricks.

It was the beginning of what would be a long year.

Throughout Greg's senior year classmates spit on him, dumped food on him, tore up his books, and pushed him down the stairs. Several students even urinated in his locker.

As far as they were concerned, anyone who associated with blacks deserved to be treated the way black people were treated back then. Such was the prevailing culture in the 1960s, especially in the South.

In 1953, when Greg was six, Greg's father—a minister—moved his family to the Koinonia Farm, a Christian commune now known as the birthplace of Habitat for Humanity. But in those days it was viewed as a den of communists and race-mixers. At Koinonia, white families and black families lived together—an unforgivable sin in the South at that time.

The KKK often targeted Koinonia during those turbulent years. Greg remembers seeing their roadside produce stand blown up with dynamite. Sometimes Klan members even fired guns from passing cars while he was playing with other kids on the farm.

But the violence and hate wasn't limited to the farm. Three white families from Koinonia, including Greg's, weren't allowed to send their children to Americus High. The Americus students and parents didn't want even the white kids from Koinonia attending their school.

The three families didn't let this go unchallenged. They sued the city schools, and a federal court ordered Americus High to enroll the students.

But the legal ruling didn't prevent discrimination. Greg's older brother couldn't take the badgering, so he transferred after one year.

Regardless of the prejudice in the South, times *were* slowly changing. By the time Greg was a senior in 1964, Americus was forced to accept a few black students. This didn't go over very well.

Greg said, "The worst part wasn't the name-calling. It was being shunned. I cut my hair like the others at the school. I dressed like them. I wanted to be their friend."

But no one wanted to be Greg's friend. He was alone. And he was the only Koinonia student left in his graduating class that senior year.

The persecution continued all year. One day some students motioned for Greg to come sit with them in the cafeteria. Greg didn't know exactly how to respond, but he figured he might as well give it a try. As he sat down, one of the guys smashed a Sloppy Joe in his face.

Most people couldn't understand why Greg continued attending Americus.

Greg still remembers the Sloppy Joe incident, because when he got home, Clarence Jordan—the Baptist minister who founded

Koinonia—saw Greg at the school bus stop and noticed the stains on his shirt. Clarence figured out what had happened, put an arm around Greg, and said something like, "This whole nonviolent thing is more an adult idea. I wonder just how much it extends to young people's lives. Maybe the best thing to do is—the next time one of those guys does something to you, just beat him up."

Greg was surprised that he was getting permission from a minister to fight back. He was tempted to fight, he admits today, but he decided that those students were just doing what they'd been taught. He told Clarence, "They are them because of their parents, and I am me because of my parents. If we'd been switched in our cribs, we'd be playing opposite roles."

Greg's decision to not fight back would be tested again.

A football player picked a fight with Greg, falsely accusing him of tripping him and calling him names. This player challenged him to a fight after school. As Greg left the campus after school, about a dozen of these guys surrounded him and began encouraging the football player to beat up Greg.

One boy kicked the books out of Greg's hands, and then the football player hit him directly in the face.

Greg didn't react the way they expected. He just stood there, waiting for the next punch. Greg was a living example of Jesus' instruction to "turn the other cheek."

Joseph Logan, a student who witnessed the encounter—now a teacher in Enterprise, Alabama—said, "I saw a sermon that afternoon."

That sermon was the beginning of a gradual change in the hearts of a few of the students.

On graduation day Greg was booed when he received his diploma. When the ceremony was over he was chased off the school grounds with rocks.

But Greg never forgot one graduate who shook his hand that day and told him, "I don't see how you made it through."

"That one act showed me there was a glimmer of hope," Greg says.

The graduate was David Morgan.

Forty years later David Morgan was the organizer of the 40th class reunion, and when he brought up the idea of inviting Greg, everyone on the reunion committee agreed that they should try to reach out to him. David wrote Greg a letter. He said later, "That was a very tough letter for me to write."

The letter began, "I expect you will be quite surprised to hear from me. If you remember me at all, it will likely be for unpleasant reasons." The letter continued. "Throughout the last 40 years, I have occasionally thought of you and those dark days that you endured at our hands. As I matured, I became more and more ashamed, and wished that I had taken a different stand back then."

When Greg got home from the post office with the letter, he said to his wife, "You won't believe this. Something wonderful is happening."

The next day when Greg went to get his mail there were three more letters in his mail box. On his drive home, he couldn't wait, so he pulled off the road and read the letters.

One of the letters was from a girl he had a crush on 40 years before.

"I will never again say, 'How could the Holocaust have happened—how could all those Christian people in Poland and Germany have stood by and allowed it to happen?' I was present with you over a long period of time, and I never once did one thing to comfort you or reach out to you. It was cruelty."

Greg stared at her letter and cried for more than 15 minutes.

Maybe things were finally changing.

Greg has done rather well since his days at Americus High. He and his wife Anne own a home on 80 acres with a view of the Greenbrier River Valley in West Virginia. His business of dealing in mountain property has put him in a financial position to retire at age 59 if he wants to.

But when the letters came, he wasn't thinking of retirement— he was talking about his days at Americus High. Greg and Anne looked through old pictures and his senior portrait in the yearbook with the caption: "He shows his true nature in what he does."

Greg admits that the past haunts him. "For years, I couldn't talk about this without a bubble of tears welling up inside."

Eleven classmates wrote Greg Wittkamper to express their regret and invite him to the reunion. While he was advised to pack a gun to the reunion by some of the students who left the school before graduation in 1965, Greg phoned the letter-writers and was convinced of their sincerity. So in June 2005 Greg and Anne attended the reunion.

They were nervous about their first stop. The initial class meeting was held at the home of Gladys Crabb, an English teacher—someone who always felt for Greg and who encouraged the reconciliation. Most of the students who wrote to Greg were at the house that day. Greg didn't know what to expect, but the group greeted him with hugs.

No one had a dry eye as they joined hands in prayer and sat down for lunch together. It had been four decades since they'd seen Greg, and they were relieved to see that he appeared to be fine. "We were all concerned that we'd really done some damage to you," said Deanie Fricks, who drove up from Naples, Florida.

As Greg shared with his old classmates, he confessed that it had taken some time to get over his anger. He said that in years past he had a recurring nightmare that he was back in high school fighting against his persecutors. "I'm standing there with a Thompson machine gun mowing down the bunch of you," he admitted honestly. It was quiet at the table as he shared that story. But Greg went on.

During one nightmare years ago, he told them, he woke and felt his resentment evaporate. He let it go. And he never dreamed of revenge again.

For Greg, it was easier to just forgive.

Greg was thankful for his upbringing. He was thankful his parents had raised him to not only love everyone, but to forgive. As a matter of fact, Greg said frankly that if it weren't for the way his parents raised him, "we could have had a Columbine on our hands."

TRANSITION STATEMENT:

We've seen the results of that kind of revenge on classmates in recent history. But by God's grace, Greg won't be in any history books. Greg found the miracle of a new beginning, and he found it in his heart to forgive.

Greg forgave his oppressors at the end of one of his nightmares. He found peace years before they even invited him to the reunion. For his classmates, healing didn't arrive until the reunion. After 40 years his classmates made an effort to reconcile. When forgiveness took place, Greg and his classmates experienced the miracle of a new beginning.

APPLICATION AND SCRIPTURE:

How about you? Do you need to experience a miracle of a new beginning? The Bible tells us in Ephesians 4:32, "Be kind and compassionate to one another, forgiving each other, just as in Christ God forgave you."

God commands us to forgive because it's the best way to live. God commands us to forgive because he has forgiven us. God is the Great Forgiver. But God also commands it because the miracle of forgiveness is the only way to be free from bitterness. To not forgive is to create another Columbine. To not forgive is to remain a prisoner of the hurt as long as you live. If I refuse to forgive, then I allow the person or people who hurt me to keep me in bondage—in chains for the rest of my life.

But when I forgive, I'm free. I'm free of my bitterness.

Sometimes the people I forgive ask to be forgiven. When that happens, I have the potential to experience the miracle of healing and restoration. That was the case with Greg, even though it took 40 years. Sometimes, though, people don't ask to be forgiven. Sometimes people don't say they're sorry. If enough time has gone by, perhaps they even forget the pain they caused. But we can still experience the miracle of healing as Greg did when he let his bitterness go.

On his own, Greg had experienced the miracle of a new beginning.

CLOSING:

I'm going to pray. Let's take a minute and close our eyes and look totally at ourselves. Ask God, "Is there someone I need to forgive?" Maybe a parent? Maybe a friend? Ask God to give you the miracle of a new beginning right now as you forgive that person.

Let's pray.

Source: Jim Auchmutey, *The Atlanta Journal-Constitution*, October 22, 2006

TALK 11
TITLE: THE SHOPPING CART

TOPIC: Giving God Total Control

BIG IDEA: We need to give God total control.

SCRIPTURE:

> "I have been crucified with Christ and I no longer live, but Christ lives in me. The life I now live in the body, I live by faith in the Son of God, who loved me and gave himself for me."
> (Galatians 2:20)

PARTICULARS:

This story is from the creative mind of my friend Matt Furby. Matt told it as a personal story, and I think everyone in the room related when they heard it—I know I could. If this story happened to you as a kid, then I encourage you to tell it in the first person.

THE STORY:

Michael's trips to the grocery store with his mom were a big part of growing up. As a small child, Michael always got to ride in the grocery cart. He loved this little seat in the front of the cart. It put kids in a great position to pull things off shelves that they couldn't reach from the ground. Michael's mom constantly found things in the cart that she never put in there. *Let's see—peanut butter, bread, milk...Mr. Wiggley's Invisible Decoder Ring?*

One day Michael grew too big to ride in the shopping cart. Something happens when you can no longer ride in the cart. If you can't ride, you want something else. If Michael couldn't be in it, he wanted to *drive* it!

Every kid wants to drive the shopping cart. Just look at it. It's got four wheels, that big handle that you can grip like a motorcycle, and that little bar across the bottom that you can put your feet up on and coast when you're going fast enough. It's a kid's dream toy.

Unfortunately, Michael never got the chance. Like all moms, Michael's mom always controlled the cart. When she would step away from the cart to reach for some Wheaties on a high shelf or lean over for some frozen peas in one of those frozen food bins, he'd try to take control and push the cart. She always caught him and quickly objected. "No, I've got the cart. I don't want you running into somebody!"

Michael always hated that. "Like I would," he'd mumble to himself.

This happened for years. She'd abandon the shopping cart for a moment and Michael would grip the controls (not that shopping carts have controls—but he always pretended). She always intervened immediately. Nothing mean, nothing harsh, just, "Sorry, honey, I've got it."

Eventually it became a regular discussion. "Mom, when can I drive the cart?"

"When you're older."

Always when I'm older, Michael thought. She never indicated when *older* was; it was obviously just older than that particular moment, because she wouldn't budge.

This didn't stop him from asking. Michael asked every time he visited the grocery store. "Mom, can I drive the cart now?"

"No, honey, not this time."

"Mom, can I drive the cart now?"

"No, honey, not this time."

"Mom, can I drive the cart now?"

"No, honey, not this time."

It was hopeless. He figured he'd probably get his driver's license before he could drive the stupid shopping cart.

But one day, Michael's hopes were lifted. He almost missed it because he was expecting the same ol' thing. He entered the grocery store and his mom did her usual routine: Walking to the cart pit and testing which one was the cleanest and had well-balanced wheels. When she selected the best cart he asked the usual question: "Can I drive the cart now?"

That's when she surprised him with her response. She didn't give the usual retort. She paused, looked at him, and smirked a little. "Sure, you can have control."

His jaw hit the ground. He couldn't believe it. He'd been waiting for this moment for years. It was finally here. He was finally *older*. He was actually going to get to drive the cart. He was going to be the one in control. After all, that's what she said: *Sure, you can have control.* That was all Michael needed. It was an oral contract, upheld in a court of law. Michael was promised control.

She stepped to the side of the cart as he walked up to the "driving" position. He placed his hands on the smooth, red plastic surrounding the handle and held it the way a biker on a Harley would grip. He was finally going to be in control. His mom was going to let him be in control.

Then she did it.

No sooner had Michael gripped the plastic—only a millisecond had gone by—than his mother maneuvered to the side of the cart, placed her left hand on the edge of the cart, and resumed control, guiding its direction.

Michael was livid. She'd said that Michael could have control, but she'd lied! She had acted as if Michael would be the driver. She implied he would have control. But it was just a ploy to make him *think* he had control. He didn't have control. She had control. He had about as much control as the driver on the Indiana Jones ride at Disneyland. Michael controlled nothing!

TRANSITION STATEMENT:

Don't you hate that?

I do. I hate it when someone tells me I can have control but doesn't let go.

If someone isn't planning to give us control—why would she lie and tell us we *can* be in control?

We do that to God all the time.

APPLICATION AND SCRIPTURE:

We tell God he can have control of our lives, but then we don't let go and let God drive. We still don't trust the direction God's going, so we keep our hands on the controls. We're afraid to give God total control.

God wants to drive. And ironically, though God's a much better driver than we are, we still have trouble giving up control.

We need to give God total control. This requires trusting God. This takes faith. We can't live the way we want—we need to let God live in us the way he wants.

The Bible talks about this in Galatians 2:20 when it says, "I have been crucified with Christ and I no longer live, but Christ lives in me. The life I now live in the body, I live by faith in the Son of God, who loved me and gave himself for me."

We need to give up total control. That means letting go of the controls and trusting God to drive...in every area of our lives.

CLOSING:

I'm going to pray. Let's take a minute and close our eyes. I encourage you to not think about the person to your right or to your left.

Just take a few seconds and think about who really has control of our lives. Have we given control to God? Or are we holding on? Maybe some of us need to relinquish control tonight.

Let's pray.

TALK 12
TITLE: MOTIVATED

TOPIC: Focus on Christ

BIG IDEA: Fix your eyes on Jesus.

SCRIPTURE:

> "Therefore, since we are surrounded by such a
> huge crowd of witnesses to the life of faith, let us
> strip off every weight that slows us down, especially
> the sin that so easily hinders our progress. And let us
> run with endurance the race that God has set before
> us. We do this by keeping our eyes on Jesus . . ."
> (Hebrews 12:1-2, NLT 1996)

PARTICULARS:

This is the inspiring true story of Olympic gold medalist Wilma Rudolph. It has a good number of details to memorize, so you'll want to spend a little more time rehearsing this one than the others.

THE STORY:

A small girl hobbled across the yard with leg braces attached to her crooked leg, her left foot twisted inward. Neighborhood kids laughed and pointed. They couldn't have guessed that this young girl would grow up to be the "fastest woman in the world" at the 1960 Rome Olympics.

This girl was Wilma Rudolph, and Wilma wasn't one to let her disability hold her back. Wilma became the first American woman to win three gold medals in one Olympics. She won the 100-meter and 200-meter races and anchored the U.S. team to victory in the 4x100-meter relay, breaking records along the way.

But it wasn't an easy journey. Her story is amazing.

Wilma was born prematurely, weighing only 4½ pounds at birth. She was sick most of her childhood, suffering from double pneumonia, scarlet fever, and polio. After losing the use of her left leg at six, she was fitted with metal leg braces.

"I spent most of my time trying to figure out how to get them off," she said. "But when you come from a large, wonderful family, there's always a way to achieve your goals."

Wilma was one of 22 children from her father's two marriages. She got her brothers and sisters to serve as lookouts while she removed her braces, forcing herself to learn to walk without them.

Wilma's disability affected her family. Her brothers and sisters took turns massaging her crippled leg every day. For years Wilma underwent weekly therapy, requiring her mother to drive 90 miles roundtrip to a Nashville hospital. Although these rides would've robbed most young people of their determination, Wilma refused to give up her dream of not only running and jumping like a normal kid, but of becoming an athlete. She was determined not to allow her disability to get in the way of her vision.

Wilma was fortunate to have a Christian mother who often said to her, "Honey, the most important thing in life is for you to believe it and keep on trying."

By the time Wilma reached her 11th birthday, she had shed those braces and was playing basketball with her brothers in the yard. "After that," her mother said, "it was basketball, basketball, basketball."

Wilma's older sister, Yvonne, was quite good at basketball, so Wilma began to play with her. When Yvonne and Wilma tried out for the school basketball team, Wilma didn't make the cut. But their father made a decision that would be pivotal in Wilma's life. He made Wilma go to all the games, feeling that Yvonne needed a chaperone. Because Wilma traveled with the team, she got to know the coach—and one day she got the courage to issue him this challenge: "If you will give me 10 minutes of your time every day, only 10 minutes, I'll give you a world-class athlete."

The coach took Wilma up on her challenge and she won a starting position on the all-African-American Burt High School girls' basketball team, where her coach, C.C. Gray, gave her the nickname "Skeeter."

"You're little, you're fast, and you always get in my way," he said. Rudolph became an all-state player, setting a Tennessee state record of 49 points in one game.

When basketball season ended, she decided to try out for the track team. That decision turned out to be one of the most significant of Wilma's life. It started when Wilma beat her girlfriend in a race. Then she beat every girl in her high school. Soon, she beat every girl in the state of Tennessee.

Wilma was only 14 years old, but she'd come a long way since her leg braces.

Ed Temple, the Tennessee State track coach, made a visit to Wilma's high school to see her run. He couldn't believe her natural ability. When he asked her about it, she said, "I don't know why I run so fast. I just run."

She loved running so much she started attending Temple's daily practices at Tennessee State. Eventually, while still in high school, she was invited to join the Tigerbelles track team.

Temple, also a sociology professor at Tennessee State, was a tough coach—dedicated to his team. As coach, a volunteer position, Temple drove the team to meets in his own car and had the school track—an unmarked and unsurfaced dirt oval—lined at his own expense. But Temple was not a pushover. He made the girls run an extra lap for every minute they were late to practice. Wilma made the mistake of oversleeping practice by 30 minutes one day and she had to run 30 extra laps. She was 30 minutes early the next day.

Wilma continued winning short dashes and the 440-yard relay. Two years later she was invited to try out for the Olympics. At 16, Wilma qualified and ran in the 1956 games in Melbourne,

Australia. She won a bronze medal—her team placed third in the 400-meter relay.

The victory was bittersweet. Yes, she'd made the Olympics and won a medal; but in her own eyes Wilma had only won the bronze. She wanted the gold. She decided to try again in four years.

Wilma knew that if she wanted to win the gold, she'd have to dedicate an enormous amount of time, commitment, and discipline. Wilma started daily training runs at 6 a.m., 10 a.m., and 3 p.m. She'd often sneak down the dormitory fire escape from 8 to 10 p.m. to get in some running on the track before bed. For more than three years—a total of more than 1,200 days—Wilma maintained this punishing schedule.

Finally 1960 arrived.

The Rome Olympics was her stage. When Wilma walked out on the field, she was prepared. This would be her day.

She was thrilled as 100,000 fans began to chant, "Vilma, Vilma, Vilma!" as they sensed her spirit of victory.

She didn't disappoint them. She tied the world record of 11.3 seconds in the semifinals then won the final by three yards in 11 seconds flat. But because of a 2.75-meter per second wind—above the acceptable limit of two meters per second—she didn't receive credit for a world record.

In the 200, she broke the Olympic record in the opening heat in 23.2 seconds and won the final in 24.0 seconds. In the relay, Wilma, despite a poor baton pass, overtook Germany's anchor leg—and the Americans, all women from Tennessee State, took the gold in 44.5 seconds after setting a world record of 44.4 seconds in the semifinals.

Wilma became the highlight of the event. Ed Temple was quick to remind reporters that there were three other gold medalists on the platform with Rudolph during the relay event. Almost the entire 1960 Olympic team, coached by Temple, came from his Tennessee State team.

After the Olympics, when the team competed in Greece, England, Holland, and Germany, it was the charming Rudolph whom fans wanted to watch perform. *Sports Illustrated* reported that mounted police had to keep back her admirers in Cologne. In Berlin, fans stole her shoes, then surrounded her bus and beat on it with their fists until she waved.

"She's done more for her country than anything the U.S. could have paid her for," Temple said. In her soft-spoken, gracious manner, Wilma paved the way for African-American athletes to follow.

Buford Ellington, the governor of Tennessee, was known for being an old-fashioned segregationist. When he decided to head up her victory celebration in her hometown, Wilma refused to attend because it was a segregated event. That's how Wilma's victory celebration—a parade and banquet—became Clarksville, Tennessee's first integrated event.

Among the many young African-American female athletes Wilma inspired was a young track star, Florence Griffith Joyner. Florence was the next woman to win three gold medals in one Olympics, doing so in the 1988 games. Jackie Joyner-Kersee's husband and coach, Bob Kersee, believed Wilma Rudolph was the single greatest influence for African-American athletes.

"She was always in my corner," said Joyner-Kersee, winner of six Olympic medals. "If I had a problem, I could call her at home. It was like talking to someone you knew for a lifetime."

But Wilma's influence didn't end after the Olympics. She was a mother of four children, a track coach at Indiana's DePauw University, and the U.S. goodwill ambassador to French West Africa. She also created a not-for-profit, community-based amateur sports program, the Wilma Rudolph Foundation.

A little more than a decade after the 1960 Olympics, Wilma Rudolph was voted into the Black Athletes Hall of Fame (1973) and the National Track and Field Hall of Fame (1974). In 1977 NBC made a movie about her life titled "Wilma." Denzel Washington played her boyfriend in his first movie role.

On November 12, 1994, Wilma died of brain cancer at the age of 54. One of her 1960 Olympics teammates, Bill Mulliken, summed up her life the best: "She was beautiful, she was nice, and she was the best."

TRANSITION STATEMENT:

Winning the gold takes motivation.

The word *motivation* is synonymous with the name Wilma Rudolph.

As a child Wilma was motivated to walk. As a young girl she was motivated to run and play. As a teenager she was motivated to win.

Wilma never took her eyes off her dream. The odds were against her, but she fixed her eyes on her goal.

What are you fixing your eyes on?

APPLICATION AND SCRIPTURE:

When it comes to following Christ, sometimes we become easily distracted. The apostle Paul talks about this struggle in the book of Hebrews:

> "Therefore, since we are surrounded by such a huge crowd of witnesses to the life of faith, let us strip off every weight that slows us down, especially the sin that so easily hinders our progress. And let us run with endurance the race that God has set before us. We do this by keeping our eyes on Jesus . . ."
> (Hebrews 12:1-2, NLT 1996)

I love the word the New Testament uses for *race*—it means "agony" (*agnon* in the original Greek). A race isn't something people just do. They don't wake up one day and say to themselves, "I think I'll run a race." A race is demanding. Often it's grueling and agonizing. That's why the verse uses the word *endurance*. We need to keep it up at all costs.

Wilma was an example of this. She never lost sight of her goal. She strove toward it with endurance.

What's the key?

The key for Wilma was her focus on her goal. And the key for us is where we focus. That's why the verse talks about keeping our eyes on Jesus.

When we fix our eyes on Jesus, we're motivated. When we remember what he did for us (dying and rising again, forgiving us, enabling us, loving us), that is the great motivation.

Think of that day when Jesus will say to you, "I know you loved me—thank you for your love and devotion. You are a winner."

CLOSING:

As you think about Wilma Rudolph, the many Old Testament winners of Hebrews 11, and about Jesus, pray with me that God will help you get rid of distractions and keep your eyes on the prize.

Let's pray.

Source: ESPN.com, "Rudolph Ran and the World Went Wild," M.B. Roberts, special to ESPN.com.

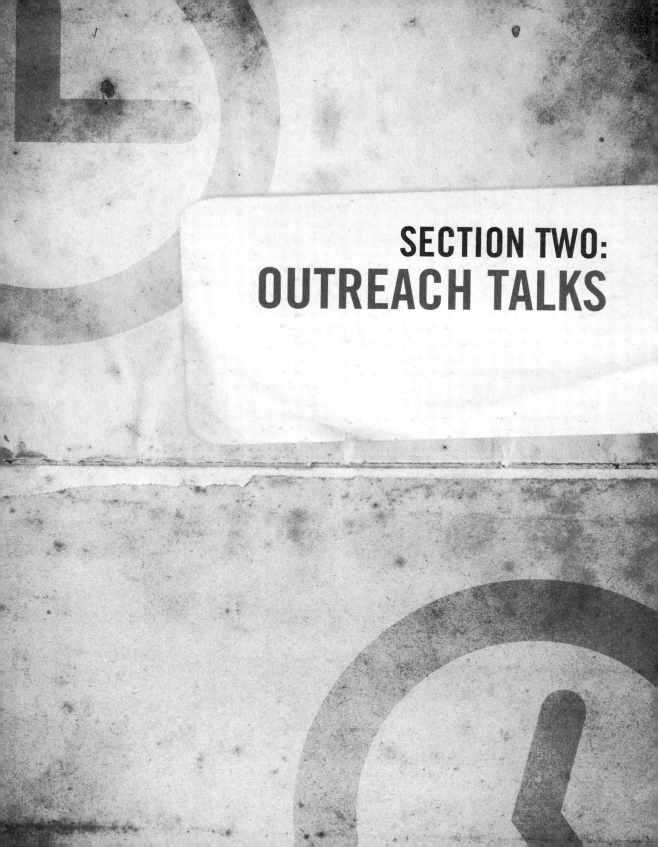

SECTION TWO:
OUTREACH TALKS

TALK 13

TITLE: A NEW BEGINNING

TOPIC: Clean Slate

BIG IDEA: God cares more about our future than our past.

SCRIPTURE:

> "'…Then neither do I condemn you,' Jesus declared. 'Go now and leave your life of sin.'" (John 8:11)

PARTICULARS:

This young woman's story is true and powerful, but I changed the names and small details for anonymity. It's a great story to help kids not only consider their day-to-day choices but also realize it's not too late to make a change.

THE STORY:

The only thing worse than dying of AIDS is living with AIDS. Donna has been living with AIDS for almost a decade.

Donna's friends from high school wouldn't even recognize her now. Her body has taken a beating for the last eight years. Her hair is cut shorter for easier care, and her weight has dropped to a level that leaves her looking as frail as a woman three times her age.

Donna never knows when she'll get sick. She'll feel great one moment, and the next moment she'll be sick to her stomach. At times, while she shopped at the mall, she lost control of her bowels. She has a few close friends who come to get her at times like these, bringing her home and helping her clean herself up.

Donna never would've guessed this is how her life would turn out. She was a popular student in high school and very pretty. Like most of her friends, she frequented parties and tried drinking—and even a little pot. It never even occurred to her that she'd become an alcoholic. She never considered the possibility that she'd wake up with guys she didn't even know. And AIDS was never a fear. In Donna's mind, AIDS was never even a possibility.

But Donna's drinking became more regular and her partying became more severe. The more she partied, the more reckless her behavior became. She doesn't even remember the first time she had sex—she couldn't tell you his name.

Donna's drinking led to other substance abuse. Donna was living her life for herself, and she figured she'd be happiest doing whatever she wanted. That was her philosophy in life: *Do whatever I want, and take it one day at a time.*

By the time Donna would've graduated from high school, she'd dropped out, was kicked out of her house, and found herself sleeping with people for alcohol or drugs. But this wasn't enough to support her habit, so she began robbing houses with some of her friends.

This went on for several years. Donna would sometimes wake up on a sidewalk somewhere on a street she didn't recognize. Then this became a regular occurrence—she was homeless.

One day Donna woke up on someone's front lawn in the suburbs. She had no idea where she was—she couldn't even remember the night before. But her eyes opened to see a well-dressed older couple standing over her. "Are you okay, young lady? Should we call an ambulance?"

Donna quickly waved them away. "I'm fine. Sorry, I just felt sick and had to lie down for a few minutes."

But the couple didn't go away. They insisted she come inside their house and get something to eat.

Donna says she was thinking, *This is great! I'll get a free meal out of these idiots and stake out their house so I can come and rip them off later.*

This became an easy possibility because the couple fed her eggs and some delicious hot blueberry muffins, then told her they needed to leave for church. They invited Donna, but she refused: "Sorry. I don't do church." She started to get up to leave, but the couple insisted she stay for a while.

"We'll be back in just a couple of hours. Make yourself at home." The man put on his coat and the lady disappeared into the bedroom for a moment.

Donna thought to herself, *These Christians could be the stupid-est people in the entire world. They have no idea who they just invited into their house.*

The lady brought Donna a blanket, tucked her in on the hide-a-bed in the living room, and left for church with her husband.

Donna was pretty tired, so she thought she'd catch a quick nap, then rip these people off when she woke up.

Donna awoke to the smell of something delicious. She opened her eyes and saw the Christian lady darting around the kitchen in an apron. Donna was a little bummed that she'd overslept, but she thought she'd wait it out and see what happened.

The lady brought her lunch: Pot roast, mashed potatoes, gravy, and hot, fresh chocolate chip cookies. The three of them sat there and talked. The couple was probably about the age of Donna's parents, she figured. But she hadn't seen them in years—ever since she was kicked out of the house. To this day, the last image she remembers of them is her mom crying in the living room and her dad calling the locksmith to change the locks. Donna didn't blame them. She had sold about $2,500 worth of her mom's jewelry at a pawnshop.

But this couple was different. They were nice, not very invasive, and the woman was a really good cook.

Day turned to evening and the couple invited Donna to stay the night. Donna gladly accepted and went to bed figuring that she would rip off these stupid people—nice, but stupid—in the morning.

One day turned to two. Days turned to weeks and weeks into months. The hospitality continued and so did the invitations to church. Donna always kindly refused church but accepted the hospitality. And this couple continued to offer hospitality despite her resistance to church attendance.

Donna still partied with her friends, but now she had a place to sleep if she needed it. She kept coming back. Every night as she went to bed, she figured she'd probably rip them off the next day. But she never did.

One Saturday afternoon Donna sat in the kitchen watching the lady make a coffee cake. Donna began asking questions, and the questions turned into a conversation about God and the meaning of life. The lady had never been pushy about God or church, and she wasn't at this moment. She just shared what she believed. She explained that God had changed them and was still changing them for the better every day. Donna asked more about this relationship with God. The lady shared that it gave her meaning and fulfillment. Donna had never had either of those things, but she longed for them—and in all honesty, if these people had this relationship with God, that was good enough for Donna. These were the nicest people she'd ever met. She figured that if God was anything like these people, then that was a pretty cool God.

Thirty minutes later Donna got on her knees on the mustard-yellow linoleum and prayed with her new friend. With the sweet smell of brown sugar in the kitchen air, Donna gave her life to Christ.

Donna began going to church and learning about this new relationship with God. She learned about the Bible and praying. She learned more about Jesus and the sacrifice he made. Donna even began memorizing Scripture and attending a women's Bible study at the church.

Six months passed. Donna was sober and drug-free. She hadn't attended a party since her commitment.

But one weekend the couple traveled out of town to visit relatives. Donna stayed—and found the house quiet and depressing when it was empty. At that unfortunate time, the phone rang. It was one of her partying buddies from six months earlier when she was partying, too, while living at this house. Her friend invited her to come party, and Donna initially refused. But her friend kept pressing, and Donna figured it wouldn't hurt. She could just enjoy the social element of the party and not return to her old habits.

Donna saw all her old friends at the party. It was a life she thought she'd left behind, but she missed her friends and enjoyed the energy of the party. She had a drink or two, and before she knew it, she was on her sixth drink.

One thing led to another, and Donna did some things that she swore she'd left behind. And that night—that one night—Donna got AIDS.

TRANSITION STATEMENT:

Some of us have a past that haunts us. Maybe not a past like Donna's, but a past nevertheless. The crazy thing is that often kids think, "If I've blown it once, it's too late now. I've already blown it, so who cares what I do now?"

Let me tell you the truth. It's not too late for a new beginning. Donna had done every bad thing in the book, and God still poured out grace on her. There's nothing we can do that separates us from the love of God. In all of Donna's wrongdoings, she was miraculously given a fresh start—a new beginning.

You have that right now. You have a new beginning. Whatever you've done before you walked in that door tonight is behind you. You have your life ahead of you. It's not too late.

APPLICATION AND SCRIPTURE:

In John chapter 8 Jesus meets a woman who might have been much like Donna. This woman had just been caught in the act of adultery. Some of the religious people of the day tried to find out how Jesus would respond to a woman caught in this kind of sin. Jesus simply told them, "Let any one of you who is without sin be the first to throw a stone at her." (v. 7)

No one was sinless—they all knew it—so they all left until just Jesus and the woman were standing there.

Jesus straightened up and asked her, "Woman, where are they? Has no one condemned you?"

"No one, sir," she said.

"Then neither do I condemn you," Jesus declared. "Go now and leave your life of sin." (vv. 3-11)

CLOSING:

Donna and this woman ⬚
turned to her life of sin, ⬚
woman responded.

How will you respond ⬚

Why don't you all close ⬚
about yourself for a mom⬚

Tonight, God cares a ⬚
about your past. It doesn'⬚
tonight, but it does matter ⬚

You've been given a s⬚
Sure, you're not going to be perfect. I'm sure Donna wasn't perfect during those six months. But she left her life of sin because she knew how empty that life was.

God has given you a fresh start. You can take this opportunity for a new life, or you can return to your old ways. It's your choice, and no one can make it for you.

Let's pray.

TALK 14

TITLE: THE AMERICAN DREAM—OR WAS IT?

TOPIC: Satisfaction in Christ

BIG IDEA: Money can't satisfy the deepest part of our lives.

SCRIPTURE:

> "Not that I was ever in need, for I have learned
> how to be content with whatever I have. I know how
> to live on almost nothing or with everything. I have
> learned the secret of living in every situation, whether
> it is with a full stomach or empty, with plenty or little.
> For I can do everything through Christ, who gives me
> strength." (Philippians 4:11-13, NLT 2004)

1 Tim. 6:6, 8
Heb 13:5
Pr. 19:23

PARTICULARS:

This true story is reinforced by the fact that it's *not* the only one of its kind. I find that when most kids hear the beginning of this story, they don't want to believe it could happen to them. They want to believe that money equals happiness. They want to believe this story is an exception to the majority. That's why I love the statistics at the end of the story—a powerful wake-up call to a materialistic generation of young people.

THE STORY:

Buying a lottery ticket.

Sounds like a pretty simple way to get rich. Many of the lottery jackpots are multimillion-dollar prizes. That's a lot of cash. Maybe that's why so many millions of people buy lottery tickets with every paycheck. It would solve all their problems, erase all their worries, fulfill most of their dreams—or would it?

Billy Bob Harrell, Jr. thought the lottery was his answer. In June 1997 he got his wish. He was doing his normal routine—glancing over the Sunday paper and checking his Quick Pick numbers—when his heart skipped a beat. He looked twice at the numbers, reading them again. He even called to his wife Barbara Jean to double-check the numbers.

The numbers didn't lie. He won the Texas jackpot of $31 million.

Billy Bob was ecstatic. His dreams had come true.

He immediately thanked God for this gift, feeling God had sent it as an answer to his problems. The last couple of years had been very difficult for Billy Bob—he'd been laid off from several jobs. He finally got a job stocking shelves at Home Depot, but that was hardly enough income to provide for his family of five.

He wanted to do so much more for his children, so every Wednesday and Saturday he purchased a couple of lottery tickets. If he wasn't using the kids' birthdates for his selection, he would let the Quick Pick computer system pick the number. The state's computer system chose the number that made Billy Bob a millionaire.

Adios, Home Depot. Billy Bob was done stocking shelves.

About a month after the winning numbers were announced, the five Harrells, their minister, and Billy Bob's attorneys all arrived in Austin to collect the first of 25 annual checks for $1.24 million. Billy Bob felt that his hard times were a thing of the past. As he received his first check, he said to the media, "Life has been tough for our family, but we've survived through the worst of it. I wasn't going to give up. Everyone kept telling me it would get better, but I never realized that it would get this much better."

And life *was* much better—for a while. Billy Bob purchased the ranch he'd always wanted. He bought six homes for himself and other members of his family. He bought a new car for each of his teenagers and his wife.

Billy Bob didn't hoard it all for himself, either. He loved giving to his church. When people in the church came to him for help, Billy Bob was generous. He gave and gave. Frankly, Billy Bob was an easy touch, partly because he remembered what it meant to be poor and partly because he thought the money would never end.

But in a few months, things began to come apart. Billy Bob spent too much too fast. His giving and spending spiraled out of control. His finances weren't the only things suffering. In February the following year his marriage came apart—a marriage already strained before Billy Bob became a millionaire. He thought that the lack of money was the cause of the tension, but he quickly discovered that lots of it couldn't save his marriage.

Once he *had* the money, he was surprised to find himself just as empty as when he was poor, if not more so.

Money wasn't the answer.

Money didn't buy happiness.

Money couldn't keep his family together.

On May 22, 1999, 20 months after becoming a multimillionaire, Billy Bob went upstairs to the bedroom of his upscale Kingwood home and locked the door. He took off all his clothes, put a shotgun barrel to his chest, and pulled the trigger.

Billy Bob Harrell, Jr.'s life on this earth was over, and his fortune was gone.

The family that celebrated his winnings and received unremitting gifts not only was left without a father, husband, and son— but also without the fortune. A conflict developed between Billy Bob's children and Billy Bob's parents. The family was left with so little of the fortune they couldn't even pay the estate taxes. They all agreed: Money didn't come close to solving any of their problems.

Billy Bob attested to that. Shortly before his death, Billy Bob confessed to his financial adviser: "Winning the lottery is the worst thing that ever happened to me."

Some of us might think the lottery equals the road to the American dream. For the Harrells, it was more like a nightmare.

Was this a unique occurrence? Maybe this story is an exception to the rule. Maybe the lottery *is* the answer for most people.

Is it?

Evelyn Adams won the New Jersey lottery twice (1985 and 1986) for $5.4 million. Today the money is all gone, and Adams lives in a trailer on food stamps. Evelyn says, "I won the American dream, but I lost it, too. It was a very hard fall. It's called rock bottom."

William "Bub" Post now scrapes out a living on his $450 Social Security checks and food stamps after winning the $16.2 million Pennsylvania Lottery back in 1988. William Post says, "I wish it never happened. It was totally a nightmare. I was careless and foolish, trying to please others . . . I'm tired, I'm over 65 years old, and I just had a serious operation for a heart aneurysm. Lotteries don't mean anything to me."

Susanne Mullins is deeply in debt after winning $4.2 million in the Virginia lottery in 1993.

Ken Proxmire used the $1 million to go into the car business when he won the Michigan lottery. Within five years he was bankrupt.

William Hurt spent the $3.1 million he won in the Michigan lottery on his divorce and crack cocaine. Within two years he was broke and charged with murder.

Charles Riddle won the Michigan lottery for $1 million in 1975. His marriage came apart, he was sued by people wanting his money, and he was indicted for selling cocaine.

In 1998 Janite Lee of Missouri won $18 million, but eight years later she was bankrupt with only $700 in the bank. She was so excited about her win that she gave it away to political, educational, and community charities.

TRANSITION STATEMENT:

If only I were rich...

If only I had more...

If only...

Most of us are looking for fulfillment in life. The majority of the reality shows and commercials on TV try to convince us that money and possessions are the answer. Are they?

Does money bring fulfillment?

APPLICATION AND SCRIPTURE:

The New Testament alone contains more than 500 verses on prayer and fewer than 500 verses on faith. But there are 2,350 verses on money and possessions. Almost half of Jesus' parables are about how to handle money and possessions. Why all the focus on money?

The writers of the New Testament knew how easy it is to give in to the lure of money.

But money doesn't satisfy. It doesn't fill the deepest part of our lives—our spirits.

Do you remember Pascal's Triangle in geometry class? Pascal also has a vacuum. Not like a Hoover for your carpet—a void. Blaise Pascal, the famous French scientist, suggested that each person has a void in his life; he called it the "God-Shaped Vacuum." This vacuum can only be filled with God. Our spirit was created so it can't be satisfied with anything other than God himself.

Pascal's theory is based on truth from the Bible. The apostle Paul gives us insight on what it is to be totally satisfied in Christ when he wrote from a prison cell:

> "Not that I was ever in need, for I have learned how to be content with whatever I have. I know how to live on almost nothing or with everything. I have learned the secret of living in every situation, whether it is with a full stomach or empty, with plenty or little. For I can do everything through Christ, who gives me strength." (Philippians 4:11-13, NLT 2004)

Paul was in prison in Rome, chained to Roman guards 24/7, waiting for a trial. You'd think this would depress a guy. But Paul wasn't shaken. He was completely satisfied.

Many of us go through life trying to satisfy ourselves with temporary things like money. The sad fact is that we need so much more than money. Nothing will fill our God-shaped vacuum except God. God is what we're looking for.

You don't need to look any longer. You don't need to wonder what will fill that void in your life. God is the only thing that fills that void, and you can fill it right now. It just takes trust. That's why people call it a life of faith. You have to trust God and live for him.

CLOSING:

I'm going to pray. Let's close our eyes for a moment and think of ourselves, not those around us. And as I pray, some of you might want to pray with me and ask God to come fill that void in your life.

Sample Prayer: *God, I'm empty, and I keep trying to find my satisfaction from external stuff like possessions and money. God, forgive me for trying to live life my way, trying to find satisfaction from temporary things. I want to put my faith in you. Come into my life. I ask you this in faith, realizing that I need to trust in you, living for you, not for me.*

Sources: "Billy Bob's (Mis)Fortune," Steve McVicker, *Houston Press*, February 10, 2000; "Eight Lottery Winners Who Lost Their Millions," http://articles.moneycentral.msn.com/SavingandDebt/SaveMoney/8lotteryWinnersWhoLostTheirMillions.aspx?page=all

TALK 15

TITLE: ARE YOU HUNGRY?

TOPIC: Faith

BIG IDEA: Real faith is accompanied by action.

SCRIPTURE:

> "What good is it, my brothers and sisters, if people claim to have faith but have no deeds? Can such faith save them? Suppose a brother or sister is without clothes and daily food. If one of you says to them, 'Go in peace; keep warm and well fed,' but does nothing about their physical needs, what good is it? In the same way, faith by itself, if it is not accompanied by action, is dead." (James 2:14-17)

PARTICULARS:

This fictional story helps kids understand that faith without works is dead. Realize that this story is *not* about feeding homeless people. It's like the example James gives in the passage. The point is that faith by itself is dead.

THE STORY:

Troy hadn't planned to spend any money this morning. But as he stared down at the Wal-Mart receipt for almost $300, he really didn't care. It was the best $300 he'd ever spent.

Troy did a lot of traveling for work. On this particular day Troy was to drive up to a Milwaukee suburb for some consulting work. At just 21, Troy already worked full-time for a software development company. He had always loved computers—he networked his friends' computers together for gaming at 12. At 15 he was Microsoft certified—obviously one of the youngest to be so, because the actual application requires a driver's license number.

When Troy was 16, Hewlett Packard sought him for an internship program. Troy's skills were so superior that he landed a full-time job at 18 for $60,000 a year.

The company he now worked for sent Troy to various companies around the world to teach them and to fix and customize their software. Troy traveled to France, London, New York, and even Fresno, California.

On local trips, he drove and documented his mileage.

This was one of those trips.

Troy had left the house at 4 in the morning to be at the client's building by 9 sharp. By 7:30 a.m. he'd found the location. Troy liked to do things this way. He'd leave early, find his destination, then go out to breakfast and relax a little before showing up. It was December, so he never knew what road conditions would be like. He hated racing the clock. Unlike most of his friends, Troy wasn't one to be late.

It was 7:45 and Troy was looking for a place to eat breakfast. He pulled up to a stoplight and looked up and down the intersection. That's when he saw them.

An overweight woman and her little boy were standing back from the main road in the entry to an alley beyond the snow-covered sidewalk. What caught Troy's eye was the fact that the boy was in a dumpster, throwing something out to his mother. The boy's head would disappear and then objects would fly out like popcorn. It was rather amusing to watch.

A horn honked behind Troy. He looked up—the light was green. He accelerated and continued down the road, but he couldn't get rid of that mental picture.

A Denny's sign poked out a block ahead. Troy pulled in the driveway and parked. But he couldn't bring himself to turn off the car. He just sat there for a moment with the car running, staring at the tree in front of him. But his mind was back at that alleyway.

Troy put the car in reverse.

When Troy hung a left on the street with the alley, he drove past slowly, surveying the situation. The boy was out of the dumpster now, and he and his mom were picking through garbage on the ground and throwing it into a large plastic bag. They disappeared from view as Troy's Volvo continued down the road.

Troy pulled up to the next signal, tapping his steering wheel as he debated what to do. He knew nothing about these people. For all he knew they'd be scared or even offended if he stopped to offer help. Besides, how did he know that they even needed help?

That thought barely escaped before another voice inside him argued, "Because they were digging through the garbage, you moron!"

Troy hung a U-turn.

As he pulled up to the icy curb and rolled down his window, he realized that he had no idea what to say. He shot a quick silent prayer up to God saying, "Help me a little bit here."

As his car stopped, the boy noticed Troy and tapped his mom's shoulder. She stopped what she was doing and lifted her glance to Troy. Her face was dirty. Her thumbs poked through the ends of her sweatshirt; she'd wrapped the cuff around her hands for warmth. Some sort of scarf was wound around her head. The boy's clothes were filthy, too, and his jacket was ripped. His pants were high waters, exposing two colors of socks. His shoes were old and worn.

The awkward silence stretched a little too long for comfort. Finally he broke the silence. "Are you hungry?"

The boy quickly said, "Yes." His mom grabbed his arm and said, "Hush, boy." She looked at Troy skeptically and said, "No, thank you. We're fine."

This surprised Troy. He'd seen lots of homeless people, and when they were offered food, they never turned it down.

Troy thought for a second, then offered, "I'm going right around the corner to that Denny's restaurant. If you want some breakfast, I'm buying." He glanced at the time on his cell phone. "I'll be sitting in my car for the next 15 minutes going over my work I have here. So if you're there in the next 15 minutes, I'll buy you whatever you want."

The little boy spoke again. "Even pancakes?"

The mom put her hand on his shoulder again. "Isaac!"

Troy laughed. "Yes, Isaac. Even pancakes."

The mother looked at Troy one more time and smiled. "Thank you, sir..." She struggled with what to say. Troy interrupted, "I'll be in the parking lot. I hope to see you there."

Troy waited in the parking lot for 12 minutes before he saw little Isaac and his mother walk around the corner. He got out of his car and met them. "Shall we eat?"

The mother had a concerned look on her face. "Sir, you don't need to feel like you..."

Troy interrupted again. "I'm glad to help." A cold wind blew across the asphalt and he saw Isaac shiver. Troy forced a shiver, too. "Whew. It's cold. Let's get inside."

The hostess at Denny's gave the awkward-looking trio a stare when they walked in. Troy just said, "Three of us for breakfast, please."

When they were all seated at the table Troy reminded them, "Anything you want."

Isaac looked at the pictures on the colorful kids' menu. He

pointed out some of the pancake pictures to his mom. "Look, Mom, strawberries on this one!"

Troy handed him a bigger menu. "Here Isaac, forget that little kids' menu. You look like a growing young man. You need the big menu." Troy pointed to a full color picture of a stack of pancakes covered with strawberries. "How about them strawberries?!"

Isaac's eyes grew huge. "I want those." He licked his lips and rubbed his dirty little hands together.

Troy and Isaac's mom laughed at Isaac's expression.

An hour later Troy was looking at the clock on his cell phone. It was 8:50 and he knew he had to go.

"Thanks for the breakfast, Mr. Troy," Isaac said, wiping syrup off his face with the back of his hand.

Isaac's mom thanked Troy, too, and helped Isaac put his jacket back on. The left sleeve of the jacket was torn from shoulder to wrist. Troy looked down at Isaac's shoes once again. His right shoe had a huge hole in the front of it. Troy could see right into the shoe where Isaac's toe stuck out of his holey socks.

Troy glanced at his phone one more time and then looked up at his breakfast companions. "Hold on just a minute," he said, dialing a number and talking with a receptionist. He told one of his clients he was going to be an hour late. Troy had never been late before.

He hit "End" on his cell phone and said, "I passed a Wal-Mart on the way in. Maybe you'd like to accompany me. I just happen to have some money set aside for a new jacket—" Troy looked down at Isaac "—a new jacket for Isaac."

As Isaac and his mom got out of Troy's car in the Wal-Mart parking lot, Isaac's mom tried to brush some of the dirt off the front seat. Her clothes had left quite a few smudges.

"Don't worry about it," Troy insisted. "I get in this car all the time when my clothes are dirty. All our dirt will sort of blend together."

The three went shopping in Wal-Mart. Troy bought packages of fresh socks, and snow boots for both of them. He bought them each a new jacket, sweatshirts, and a bunch of T-shirts. Troy bought a huge camping backpack to put it all in.

The total came to a few hundred dollars. But he'd just spent more than that on a Playstation the week before. For some reason, this purchase felt a whole lot more fun.

As the three of them exited Wal-Mart, Isaac tugged on Troy's jacket. He motioned for Troy to lean down to him. Troy leaned over and Isaac put his hand up to his mouth to whisper something. "Don't worry," Isaac whispered. He looked both ways and put his hand to his mouth again. "I won't tell anyone."

Troy laughed, but then got a confused look on his face. "Tell anyone what?"

Isaac leaned close once again. "That you're an angel," Isaac offered matter-of-factly.

Troy had been called a lot of things in his life before, and "angel" sure wasn't one of them. But he reached out and gave Isaac a noogie before hugging them both goodbye and showing up to work an hour late.

TRANSITION STATEMENT:

Maybe you've never been called an angel—but when people look at you, who do they see?

Faith in God is proven by our actions.

APPLICATION AND SCRIPTURE:

The Bible talks about this in the book of James.

> "What good is it, my brothers and sisters, if people claim to have faith but have no deeds? Can such faith save them? Suppose a brother or sister is without clothes and daily food. If one of you says to them, 'Go in peace, keep warm and well fed,' but does nothing about their physical needs, what good is it? In the same way, faith by itself, if it is not accompanied by action, is dead." (James 2:14-17)

This passage isn't about helping homeless people. It's about faith. These verses illustrate what faith is like by telling the story of a person who says "I wish you well" but does nothing to make that wish come true. In other words, what good is it to say something but not mean it with our actions?

Faith isn't just saying, "I believe you, God!" with our mouths. True faith is accompanied by action. Actions are simply doing what we know to be right from God's Word to us. God might even nudge us to do these things at times through the Holy Spirit.

Troy was nudged, and he responded. He saw a need and acted. That is faith in action.

What is God nudging you to do?

> Take the time to get involved in a ministry
> Visit your grandmother
> Mow someone's lawn, wash their windows
> Babysit for someone who doesn't have the money to hire a babysitter
> Talk to someone you don't usually talk to

And remember—this is not how you earn your way to heaven. This is a demonstration that your faith has changed how you look at the world.

Some of us might need to rethink our faith. Is it really faith? Or is it dead faith?

Think about that for a second.

CLOSING:

Let's all bow our heads and close our eyes and take a few moments to think to ourselves. Don't disturb the person to your right or your left. As I pray, I want you to look deep inside yourselves. Have you ever made a commitment to Jesus? It's a commitment of faith. And faith is so much more than just saying, "I believe in you, Jesus!" and going back to our old ways. Real faith is accompanied by action. Faith without action is dead.

Some of us might need to make a commitment to action right now.

Let's pray.

TALK 16

TITLE: TWO HOUSES

TOPIC: Foundation

BIG IDEA: Living a life of disobedience is like building our house on sinking sand.

SCRIPTURE:

> "Therefore everyone who hears these words of mine and puts them into practice is like a wise man who built his house on the rock. The rain came down, the streams rose, and the winds blew and beat against that house; yet it did not fall, because it had its foundation on the rock. But everyone who hears these words of mine and does not put them into practice is like a foolish man who built his house on sand. The rain came down, the streams rose, and the winds blew and beat against that house, and it fell with a great crash." (Matthew 7:24-27)

PARTICULARS:

I stole this story from the Bible. I'm amazed at how often I tell this story to church kids and they don't realize the roots of the story until the very end. It has always been very effective at helping kids think about their spiritual foundation.

THE STORY:

Bob had a 2 p.m. appointment with a contractor. When he pulled up to the beachside parking lot, the contractor was there waiting.

Bob introduced himself and the contractor, Ron, did the same. Ron showed Bob a portfolio of pictures—all gorgeous houses near the beach.

Ron had been recommended to Bob by several sources. Ron built beautiful houses all over Florida, specializing in beachfront property. Bob had always wanted a beach house. He'd just inherited some money, and he planned on sinking everything into this house and retiring in it.

After looking at the portfolio, Bob looked up to survey the surrounding area. "So the only question I have is, *where?*"

Ron walked with Bob along a little trail that ran just above the beach on a small cliff overlooking the water. He pointed out several areas where he could build. Ron and a few other investors owned the whole area stretched out before them.

Bob was overwhelmed. "This is a tough decision. It's all so beautiful. On one hand I like the areas down by the water. We could open up our doors and run right out onto the beach." Bob turned his head toward the cliffs. "But the view from some of these cliffs is pretty sweet, too."

Bob scratched his head and then turned to Ron. "What would you do?"

Ron posed a question. "Well, do you just want a house for just a few years, or do you want it for a long time?"

"Oh, definitely a long time." Bob replied, zipping up his jacket to block the cool breeze. "I plan to retire in this house."

"Well, then I think the best decision would be to build right up there," Ron replied, pointing up to a beautiful rocky area over-looking a beach. "If you build your house up there, then it will be here long after you're gone. It's something your children and your grandchildren will enjoy."

Bob clapped his hands and rubbed them together. "Well, that only leaves one question, then. How much?"

Ron shuffled some papers and put a clean bid sheet into a clip-board. He asked Bob questions about square footage and materi-als. Bob was planning to build a huge house with a lot of extras. As Bob listed his desires, Ron jotted down some notes and did a few calculations. Soon he wrote down a large figure at the bottom of the page.

Ron held the clipboard for a second before showing it to Bob. "Now, Bob, let me warn you. Because of the huge rock on that cliff, we're going to have to do some drilling and extra foundation work. Don't get me wrong. That rock is a great foundation. It's unmov-able. But it's harder to work with. So the initial costs will be much higher." Ron showed Bob the figure.

Bob's eyes grew large when he saw the figure. He shook his head in disagreement. "I can't afford that. That's way too much!"

"Well, we could always trim down the square footage and cut a few of these extras. That would save a little bit."

Bob wasn't happy with that solution. He wanted a big beach house. He'd already set his expectations on a large house where he could do a lot of entertaining, throwing lots of parties and walking right outside to the beach.

Bob asked. "What are our other options? I don't want to cut down the square footage or the quality."

Ron shrugged his shoulders. "The only option is another location." He turned the other direction and pointed to another location closer to the beach. "That location would be much easier to build on. We wouldn't have to do as much foundation work or drilling into the rock. But the…"

"How much?!" Bob interrupted.

"Wait," Ron hesitated. "I'm not thrilled about this location because its foundation is weaker. It's so close to the sand that the dirt is probably made up of a lot of sand all through that hill. It's not as costly as drilling in the rock, but you'd have to dig pretty deep to build a foundation there."

"But deep is expensive, right?" Bob asked.

"Well, yes," Ron answered hesitantly. "But if you don't have a good foundation, you could end up with problems later."

Bob laughed. "I've seen tons of houses all along this coast on this exact type of earth. Nothing's going to happen to it."

Ron tried to talk Bob out of skimping on the foundation, but Bob dismissed his warnings. "Come on, Ron. How much?"

"Well, if we dug deep..."

Bob interrupted. "Ron, money doesn't grow on trees. How much if you dig a normal depth?"

Ron paused for a moment, then pulled out a new piece of paper, jotting some figures down. Eventually Ron wrote a figure at the bottom of the piece of paper. He held out the clipboard, showing it to Bob.

Bob smiled. "Now *that's* what I'm talking about!"

Bob went to Ron's office and filled out all the paperwork, including special waivers highlighting their discussion about the foundations. Bob signed the bottom line and wrote Ron a deposit check with a smile.

The plans were drawn, permits were submitted, and construction began within the month.

Three days after Ron and Bob's initial appointment, Ron had another appointment on the same beach with a young man named Peter. Peter had sold a company and was also looking to build a house along the beach. Like Bob, Peter had heard good things about Ron and the houses he built. Peter and Ron's conversation sounded much like the conversation on the beach just three days before.

"Where would you build if you were going to build a house on this beach?" Peter asked Ron.

Ron clarified. "Well, do you want a house for just a few years, or do you want it for a long time?"

"Oh, definitely a long time," Peter answered. "This will be the house my kids will grow up in, and Lord willing, their grandkids."

"Well, then I think the best decision would be to build right up there," Ron replied, pointing up to that same beautiful rocky area overlooking a beach. "If you built your house up there, then it will be here long after you're gone...long after your children and even your grandchildren."

Peter seemed happy with that answer. "Well, that sounds good. *How much?*"

Ron shuffled some papers once again and put a clean bid sheet into his clipboard. He asked Peter the routine questions about square footage and materials. Peter told Bob what he wanted. Ron jotted down some notes and did a few calculations. Soon, he wrote down a large figure at the bottom of the page.

Ron held the clipboard for a second before showing it to Peter, but once again clarified, "Now, Peter, let me warn you. Because of the huge rock on that cliff, we're going to have to do some drilling and extra foundation work. Don't get me wrong. That rock is a great foundation. It's unmovable. But it's harder to work with. So the initial costs will be much higher." Ron had a strange sense of déjà vu when he said this.

He showed Peter the figure.

Peter stared at the figure for a second, blinked, and looked again. Then he took a step back, looked at the property, and stroked his chin. "Wow! Don't get me wrong—I understand—but I can't afford that. It's just too much."

"Well, we could always cut down the square footage; that would save a little bit."

"Any other options?" Peter asked.

Ron sighed. "The only option is another location." He turned the other direction and pointed to another location closer to the beach. It was about 100 yards from another property with a SOLD sign. "That location would be much easier to build on. We wouldn't have to do all the foundation work and the drilling into the rock. As you can see, we're building another house down there."

"But you don't recommend that location?" Peter asked poignantly.

Ron paused for a moment and looked Peter right in the eyes. "Peter, it really depends on you. The fact is, that location down there could have foundation problems if you don't spend a bunch of extra money digging. But up there, you'll be building on a foundation that will last. It's your call."

Peter looked down at the figures on the paper for a moment then up at the location on the rock. After a moment he turned back to Bob. "It sounds to me like the decision is quite simple. What good is a house without a foundation that lasts?"

Ron took Peter back to his office. They worked the numbers, cut down on the square footage, and came up with a much simpler design that was affordable. Peter wrote a check for the deposit and went on his way. The plans were drawn, permits were submitted, and construction began that same month.

It was interesting to see the two projects being built so close together. The house on the cliffs took a long time to start. They brought in huge drilling equipment and worked on the foundation for more than a month. Then the walls emerged. The house wasn't big or gaudy by any means. It was functional with a nice layout and a great view.

Down the hill, Bob's house sprang up much more quickly. The foundation was dug quickly and easily, and then monstrous walls went up. The entire back of the house faced the beach. Floor to ceiling windows looked out toward the water. Plush carpeting, granite countertops—the detail was amazing.

As the finishing touches were being put on Bob's house, the THX people came out and hooked up surround sound throughout the house, installing a subwoofer larger than a grand piano. This house was going to be a great place for entertaining.

Because of the enormous size of Bob's house and all the foundation work on Peter's house, both houses were finished about the same time. In fact, both Bob and Peter threw housewarming parties on the same Friday night.

Bob had 30 people over. Everyone loved the house. Even though it was cold and windy, the French doors facing the beach were opened and people walked right out onto the sand. The music was loud and the huge subwoofer was pumping. It was quite a party.

Peter had a few friends over. They liked his house and had a fun time hanging out together. Everyone loved the gorgeous view.

All of a sudden, on the multiple plasma screens at Bob's house, a newsbreak interrupted the music video program. "This just in! Hurricane Bertha is coming, and boy, is it going to disrupt the seashore!"

In Peter's house, his radio was broadcasting the same warning. "Warning, this one is going to be Category 6. Anyone living on the coast might want to consider evacuation."

Peter's friends said goodbye and drove inland. When they were gone, he closed his shutters, removed the plants from his porch, and pulled his car into the garage.

Down at Bob's house, Bob was cranking up his stereo during the announcement, admiring his surround sound. "Check out the delay to those back speakers! That's awesome!" But no one heard him. They had all fled when they heard the announcement.

Bob shut the French doors and a couple of the open windows. But he returned to his stereo, where he began flipping through the channels. He eventually stopped on a station and began blasting '80s music throughout the house.

Boy, was that news announcer right. Hurricane Bertha brought a wave so huge it destroyed Bob's house in one strike. The house was easily shifted off its foundation and slapped against the nearby rocks, where it splintered and was dragged out to sea. Bob was last spotted floating on a gigantic subwoofer.

The winds blew and the rain came down. But no matter what Bertha did—Peter's house on the rock stood firm.

TRANSITION STATEMENT:

This story is actually from the Bible.

Okay, maybe not the part about the subwoofer or the plasma screens. But Jesus told a story like this to talk about our foundation.

APPLICATION AND SCRIPTURE:

Jesus tells this story in Matthew 7:

> "Therefore everyone who hears these words of mine and puts them into practice is like a wise man who built his house on the rock. The rain came down, the streams rose, and the winds blew and beat against that house; yet it did not fall, because it had its foundation on the rock. But everyone who hears these words of mine and does not put them into practice is like a foolish man who built his house on sand. The rain came down, the streams rose, and the winds blew and beat against that house, and it fell with a great crash." (vv. 24-27)

There are just two people in this story. One builds on a solid foundation. One builds on a weak, temporary foundation.

The most intriguing thing about this parable is that it doesn't matter what kinds of houses they had—they could've been a really fancy houses or simple houses. It didn't matter. What mattered were the foundations. What were they building their houses on?

What foundation are you building your house on?

Like the foolish man, we can try to pursue all the temporary stuff in the world: Money, status, material possessions, even relationships. But none of those outlast the storms of life. And let's be honest—we can't take any of those things with us when we die.

In this story, Jesus tells us how we can build a foundation that lasts. The answer is in trusting him.

Check it out. It's evident right there in the passage. It says you'll be building a solid foundation if you "hear these words" and "put them into practice." In other words, *if you do the things Jesus says.*

Why would we do that? We do that because we trust Jesus.

All through the Bible we learn that our relationship with him is based on faith. But so many people who *say* they believe in him don't really trust him. They might believe there was a Jesus, or believe there's a God, but they aren't willing to trust that his way is best.

The hard part is that people who aren't willing to put their trust in Jesus don't get to enjoy a relationship with him forever. Some of these people might even be religious followers of his who will say they knew him. But the bottom line is that they didn't trust him—because they didn't do what he said to do.

Just before he told the House on the Rock story, Jesus said:

> "Not everyone who says to me, 'Lord, Lord,' will enter the kingdom of heaven, but only those who do the will of my Father who is in heaven. Many will say to me on that day, 'Lord, Lord, did we not prophesy in your name, and in your name drive out demons and in your name perform many miracles?' Then I will tell them plainly, 'I never knew you. Away from me, you evildoers!'" (Matthew 7:21-23)

Jesus doesn't want fake religious followers. He wants people who trust him. He wants people who will hear his words in the Bible and do what they say.

CLOSING:

Some of us here tonight might relate more to the foolish man in the story. We're going through our lives building with cool, temporary stuff on weak, temporary foundations. We aren't putting Jesus' words into practice. We don't trust in him.

You can change that right now. You can be like the wise man and put your trust in him. You can give your life to him and say, "Jesus, forgive me for my past. I give you my future." Your trust in him will begin a lifelong relationship with him. It doesn't mean you're never going to make a mistake again—that's impossible. But it does mean you're going to start building your house on a foundation that lasts—a foundation of obedience built on trusting Jesus as your God.

Let's pray.

TALK 17
TITLE: MORE THAN THIS

TOPIC: Emptiness

BIG IDEA: There is so much more to life than the temporary goals and dreams we think will satisfy us.

SCRIPTURE:

> "Remember your Creator in the days of your youth, before the days of trouble come and the years approach when you will say, 'I find no pleasure in them...'" (Ecclesiastes 12:1)

PARTICULARS:

This story is the biography of the famous quarterback Tom Brady, and all the stats are true. (Judge for yourself to what degree your group as a whole will get into all of Brady's statistics—e.g., what round of the draft he was picked in or how many passes he completed in a playoff game; they'll probably fly with sports buffs... but bomb with non-buffs.) Either way, this talk will require a little more preparation to remember the statistics.

THE STORY:

Despite his love for football, Tom Brady never got his shot at playing quarterback on his winless freshman football team in San Mateo, California.

At the University of Michigan he warmed the bench for two years, wondering if he'd ever play. His anxiety became so bad that he hired a sports psychologist to help him cope with the stress.

In the 2000 NFL draft, almost 200 names were called before the New England Patriots chose him in the sixth round. And then Tom sat on the bench for almost his entire rookie year, waiting to play.

Tom told USA Today, "Throughout my football career it always has been looking up at other people."

But then things changed.

Quarterback Tom Brady has three Super Bowl Rings—so far. He was not only the youngest quarterback ever to win a Super Bowl, he won three of them before his 28th birthday. For a guy who felt like he'd spent most of his life on the bench, he sure got it done.

Thomas Edward Brady, Jr., was born in San Mateo, California, on August 3, 1977. He and his three older sisters loved sports. They played and watched sports from the time they were kids. Tom grew up watching *Monday Night Football* and was regularly taken to watch the 49ers play. At those games, Tom saw what he wanted to be: The next Joe Montana.

Tom didn't just sit around making wishes. He worked.

Tom played baseball and football growing up. At Junipero Serra High School in San Mateo (the alma mater of baseball player Barry Bonds and NFL Hall of Famer Lynn Swann), he worked out three times a day—practicing with the basketball team in the morning, running drills midday, and lifting weights at night.

Football wasn't his first sport. In 1995, Tom became an all-state catcher and was drafted by the Montreal Expos in the 18th round. But he accepted a football scholarship at the University of Michigan instead.

He spent two seasons on the bench at Michigan, waiting for his shot, including one year as an understudy for Brian Griese, future NFL quarterback, who would one day lead the Michigan Wolverines to the 1997 national championship.

Tom had front-row seats to this championship...on the bench.

He was frustrated. He'd never dreamed of doing so much bench time. He longed for some game time. He hired a sports psychologist to help him deal with some of these worries. He wanted to play, and he felt like he wasn't being given an opportunity. At one point Brady considered transferring from Michigan.

In 1998 Tom was finally given a starting slot on the Wolverines under Coach Lloyd Carr. He not only started every game that year, he led his team to a Citrus Bowl victory over Arkansas. For two years in a row he started every game. In 1999 he led his team to an overtime win in the Orange Bowl over Alabama, throwing for 369 yards and four touchdowns.

His final year at Michigan, Tom's numbers looked great for the upcoming NFL draft. But the draft didn't go as well as expected. It wasn't until the sixth round of the draft that his name came up (199th overall). The New England Patriots, who had a very solid quarterback in Drew Bledsoe, thought they'd take a chance with Brady and start developing him as a backup.

And so Brady's life on the bench continued all over again.

Determined to succeed, Tom worked hard with the Patriots, both physically and mentally. He gained 15 pounds of muscle and memorized his playbook. Despite his efforts, he warmed the bench his rookie year for the entire season except one game where he completed one pass against the Detroit Lions—a game no one noticed.

In 2001, Tom's second season with the Patriots, he showed up to training camp ready to prove himself to his coach, Bill Belichick, to his team, and to the world. He impressed Belichick enough to become second-string quarterback. If Bledsoe were injured or pulled, Tom was their man.

On September 23, 2001, during the second game of the season, Tom got his chance. Bledsoe got hit so hard in the chest by New York Jets linebacker Mo Lewis that he had to be helped off the field. Brady finished the game, losing to the Jets. But the word was that Bledsoe was going to be out most of the season.

Tom took charge. Ten games into the season the Patriots were just 5 and 5, but Tom was finally getting acclimated—and things began to change.

With win after win, the Patriots finished first in the AFC East. Tom had proved himself enough to receive an invitation to the Pro Bowl.

The playoffs wouldn't be easy. The Patriots were definitely the underdog. In their game against the Raiders, the Patriots were down by 10 points going into the fourth quarter. But Tom, throwing for 312 yards in his first playoff game, led the Patriots to a comeback, and the Patriots beat the Raiders.

Tom hit another wall in the divisional playoffs that year. He was injured in the Patriots-Steelers game. Bledsoe relieved him and the Patriots won, making them the AFC champions. The Patriots would be going to the Super Bowl. National debate ensued about who should start in Super Bowl 36. Tom had been the starting quarterback in every victory the Patriots had achieved that year—but first-string quarterback Bledsoe was only out because of an injury. And he proved himself more than effective in the game against the Steelers.

Despite the debate, coach Bill Belichick chose Tom to start in the Super Bowl.

Super Bowl 36 wasn't going to be an easy victory. The St. Louis Rams were known for their high-powered offense, so Tom needed to match them point for point. Sure enough, the game ended up being neck-and-neck until the very end. With less than two minutes remaining and a tie score of 17-17, Tom drove down the field, completing five of eight passes for 53 yards. The Patriots won by a mere field goal—and Tom, at 24, became the youngest quarterback ever to receive a Super Bowl Ring. He was voted MVP of the game.

Tom had earned the confidence of the Patriots so much by the beginning of his third season that they released Bledsoe. Unfortunately, the Patriots didn't have a great season. They didn't even make the playoffs that year. Despite their season, Tom's fame continued. People loved how cool and calm he was on the field. Regardless of the pressure, Tom always seemed to relax his teammates with his cool demeanor. *People* magazine voted Tom one of the *50 Most Beautiful People* that year.

During Tom's fourth season with the Patriots in 2003, the team came roaring back with an indomitable defense. After a slow start of 2 and 2, the Patriots pulled off a record-breaking season with 12 consecutive victories en route to the Super Bowl.

Tom led the Patriots to beat the Carolina Panthers in Super Bowl 38 with a score of 32-29, becoming the youngest quarterback ever to bring home *two* Super Bowl wins. He set the record for most completions by a quarterback in the Super Bowl (32) and was named Super Bowl MVP for the second time, flying to Hawaii to play in the Pro Bowl for the second time in three years.

In 2004 the Patriots dominated right out of the blocks. Tom helped them set an NFL record with 21 straight wins (dating from the previous year). The Patriots easily made it to the Super Bowl again.

Tom continued to amaze everyone with his determination and perseverance. One night, before he played the Pittsburgh Steelers—the NFL's best defensive team—Tom had a 103-degree temperature and had to be hooked up to an IV. Despite the odds, he played his finest game of the season. On February 6, 2005, Tom led the Patriots to victory over the Philadelphia Eagles, winning Super

Bowl 39—his third Lombardi trophy in four years. (He almost won a fourth Super Bowl in 2008, guiding the Patriots to a late touchdown and the lead, but the New York Giants took it right back in the final seconds.)

Tom had turned out to be quite a gem for the Patriots. He was an outstanding quarterback, and he was loved and respected by everyone. "There is no quarterback I would rather have," said his coach, Bill Belichick *(USA Today)*.

In 2005, Tom was on top of the world. At 28, he had three Super Bowl rings, and *Sports Illustrated* named him Sportsman of the Year.

Tom had achieved his life goal. He had everything he wanted. He was one of the greatest quarterbacks in history. He was rich. He was famous. He had three Super Bowl rings.

What more could anybody want?

But Tom was restless.

He wondered—"Is there something more?"

In October 2006, *USA Today*'s Tom Pedulla wrote, "As much as he has accomplished, Brady wants more. He is not content with either his lofty position in the game or his number of championships he has won."

But don't take it from Pedulla. Take it from the mouth of Tom himself. He was interviewed on *60 Minutes* on November 6, 2005. Steve Kroft and Tom talked about Tom's incredible achievements. In a rather candid moment, Tom asked Kroft: "Why do I have three

Super Bowl rings and still think there is something greater out there for me? I mean, maybe a lot of people would say, 'Hey man, this is what it is. I reached my goal, my dream...' Me, I think, *God, it's got to be more than this!*"

Kroft asked him, "What's the answer?"

Tom quickly replied, "I wish I knew. I wish I knew."

TRANSITION STATEMENT:

So many of us believe that if we achieve our lifetime goals, we'll be satisfied. Others believe that money or fame might be the answer. Regardless, we think we'd be truly satisfied if we had those things that we humanly value.

Then how come whenever people achieve this stuff—they always seem to want more?

Tom Brady is rich, famous, and has achieved his lifetime goal. His words? *"It's got to be more than this!"*

Is there?

Is there more than...this?

APPLICATION AND SCRIPTURE:

Tom's question is the same question that the writer of Ecclesiastes asked. The author tries everything that would seem to bring fulfillment: Partying, sex, money, philosophy, education, and power—

but with each failure he only becomes more cynical. He ends each search with the word *empty*. When the lights are turned out and he's alone, he finds that life is meaningless.

At the end of his book, he doesn't address his remarks to the retired or the aging. He addresses his remarks to the young and says,

> "Remember your Creator in the days of your youth, before the days of trouble come and the years approach when you will say, 'I find no pleasure in them...'" (Ecclesiastes 12:1)

What a summary verse for 11 chapters of searching for life's meaning! All through the book the author compares life "above the sun" to life "under the sun." Life "above the sun" is from God's viewpoint. It makes sense from God's perspective. But life "under the sun" is without God. It makes no sense. And that's what Tom Brady seems to be missing—his Creator, or life "above the sun."

What's the only thing that can fill that emptiness in your life? The author is saying that the answer to life is our creator—God. Only God can give meaning to life.

Tom Brady can have all the success, money, and fame anybody can find in this life—but without a relationship with God, he can only say, "It's got to be more than this!" And he's right. There *is* more.

How about you? Are you trying to find fulfillment in this life "under the sun"—the things that our world says bring satisfaction? What drives you? Is it fun? Sex? What do you live for? The latest gadget or car or clothes? Is it that scholarship to a prestigious college? Is it a sports scholarship or award? Is it a relationship with the only person you think can fulfill your wildest fantasy?

Do you know what the reality is? Those things become our gods. They try to fill the God-shaped vacuum in our lives, but they can't. Without God, all of it is meaningless. To be blunt—life on planet Earth without God is the pits, no matter how much we've achieved. Just ask Tom Brady.

CLOSING:

Let's pray.

Source: http://www.usatoday.com/sports/soac/2006-10-31-brady_x.htm

TALK 18

TITLE: ONE FOOT ON THE WIRE

TOPIC: Faith

BIG IDEA: We need to take a step of faith where we totally depend on God.

SCRIPTURE:

> "'Come,' he said. Then Peter got down out of the boat, walked on the water and came toward Jesus."
> (Matthew 14:29)

PARTICULARS:

This is the true story of the French tightrope walker who walked a line stretched between the two World Trade Center towers after they were first constructed.

THE STORY:

In recent years we've heard numerous stories about the end of the two World Trade Center towers (the Twin Towers). This story is about the beginning.

They'd spent all night stringing a steel cable across the 130-foot gap between the tops of the Twin Towers. As Wall Street woke up at 7 on the morning of August 7, 1974, Philippe Petit gave a 45-minute show across the high wire—dancing, jumping, lying down, and taunting the police who tried to coax him down. A quarter of a mile below, people stopped in disbelief, watching not a tightrope walker, but a dancer. He was doing tricks, bouncing up and down, actually leaping off the wire into the air.

At this time construction on the World Trade Center's Twin Towers was almost finished and facing financial disaster. The building's space was still mostly empty and criticism was running high against the billion-dollar project. But a 24-year-old Frenchman did something illegal that changed public opinion.

Surprisingly, the biggest feat wasn't the actual high-wire act. "That's what I do," Philippe says. "That part was easy." He performed spectacular acts all the time. The risky part of the feat was how he and his friends sneaked into the building, hid out all night, and strung the high wire.

At 18, Philippe was a street performer in Paris. He had a toothache one day, and while waiting in a dentist's office, he saw an article about the Twin Towers being built in New York. The article had an illustration of the project model form, and when Philippe saw it, he was captivated. He knew what he had to do.

He faked a sneeze and, bending over, he ripped out the page of the magazine. Hiding the page, he ran out of the office, totally forgetting about his toothache for another week.

For six years Philippe developed his plan. In January of 1974 he flew to New York for the first time to examine the towers in person. Up until now he'd only studied models and diagrams and perfected his high-wire skills. It was time to finalize his plan. He sneaked into the towers during construction, riding the elevators and running up staircases. On his first trip, it took him more than an hour to get to the roof, evading security guards all the way. On his second trip to the top of the towers he took his friend, Jim Moore, a photographer. When Jim heard what Philippe was going to do, he turned white and whispered, "You're insane."

Philippe went back to Paris to plan the fulfillment of his wild goal. He collected everything he could, building a huge file with facts about the towers. But soon he discovered that there was only so much preparing he could do in Paris. He had to go to the towers to collect all the necessary facts. So he returned to New York in April and hung out around the towers. He was street juggling to make a living and the people in Manhattan loved it. He actually did pretty well.

Meanwhile, at night he sneaked into the building, posing as a reporter and dodging security guards. As he was taking pictures and drawing access routes, he discovered some scary new information: On windy days, the building swayed enough to snap a steel cable between the towers. There was also a police station in the basement—he hadn't planned on that obstacle.

With all his information, he flew back to France for the final preparation. He built a scale model of the Trade Center in his room and researched the rigging of the wire that would connect the two buildings. He convinced a friend to put up the money—and finally, in May, he returned to New York for what he called his "coup." He kept changing the dates for the walk, but he finally fixed on a date: August 7, 1974.

On August 6, the day before his feat, Philippe and his motley crew of six friends took their forged ID passes, dressed as delivery men, and entered the World Trade Center. Since it was moving-in day for some of the major corporations occupying their new offices on the 82nd floor of the south tower, Philippe and his team were able to blend in. They rode the freight elevator up to the 104th floor of the south tower, where they delivered their equipment: A disassembled balancing pole, wire for rigging, 250 feet of one-inch braided steel cable, and a bow and arrow. Their inside man escorted two of the team disguised as businessmen up the north tower. But it was only 4:30 in the afternoon, so both teams hid until it was dark and they could begin their work.

Murphy's Law: Whatever can go wrong, will go wrong. Philippe and his team encountered several challenges that weren't in the plan. Across the world in Germany, one team member's wife was concerned that Philippe was going to kill himself, so she tried to call the New York Police Department and warn them to be on the lookout for anything unusual happening on the roof of the Twin Towers. Fortunately, although she kept calling, she couldn't get through.

The second unplanned event was an impromptu party thrown by some of the off-duty construction workers on the roof. Philippe and his friend hid on an eight-inch-wide I-beam for hours, waiting for the party to end.

Finally, early in the morning, Philippe's friend picked up the bow and arrow and fired a line from the north tower to the south tower. The two teams used the cover of darkness during the rest of the night rigging the wire. When the first construction crew arrived for work at 7 a.m., Philippe's team wasn't finished tightening the cable. Philippe was trying madly to work out problems with the final rigging when one of his team members gave up and quit. But by the time the freight elevator rose to the 104th floor with the construction crew, the two towers were linked together—something that would never happen again.

A little after 7 a.m., while people walked the streets to work, Philippe stepped out on the wire. Police and construction workers rushed to the rooftop.

When Philippe reached the other side end of the wire, he said it seemed as if a bunch of arms—octopus-like—were waving around, reaching for him. So he made a U-turn and started back. On the other side, more people tried to grab him and pull him back. He yelled at them, "Hey! I don't need help—I haven't finished my show!"

In his next crossing he started to show off. He presented the promenade trick—throwing the pole over his shoulder as if it were a pitchfork and taking a casual stroll home after a hard day working in the fields. Then he saluted the crowd, sat down, lay down, and even jumped in the air. When he looked at the end of the wire, he noticed that the men reaching out to grab him were in police uniforms. They had a French translator yelling at him to get off the wire and threatening to send a helicopter or even loosen the wire if he didn't "get off right now!"

But how do you get a guy off a high wire when almost 100,000 people on the ground are cheering for him?

To this day, no one agrees how long Philippe was on the cable. Some say he crossed six times, some say eight. Some say he was on the wire 45 minutes, others say an hour. But when he was done, Philippe decided he'd finished his act. It was time to give himself up to the police and be arrested. His coup was complete. Six years of preparation and it was all over. He had reached his goal. So he walked over to the south tower, and in the words of Philippe, "The octopus grabbed me violently."

When arrested he explained, "When I see two oranges, I juggle; when I see two towers, I walk."

Philippe immediately became one of the most famous men in the world. His picture appeared on the front page of most newspapers. He was a folk hero, and because of the overwhelming outburst of public praise, all formal charges against him were dropped. His only sentence was to perform his high-wire act for a group of children in Central Park.

The next day Richard Nixon had to resign from office because of the Watergate cover-up. Before leaving Washington by helicopter, Nixon met the press and said, "I wish I had the publicity that Frenchman had." "The Frenchman" had broken the law and was a hero.

The results of Philippe's new fame were abundant. His phone rang with every offer you can imagine. Publishers wanted him to write a book called *How to Walk the Wire in Your Back Yard in Five Days*. Burger King even offered him $100,000 to dress up as a Whopper and wire-walk across 8th Avenue to open a new franchise. He became friends with famous people like Robin Williams, Al Pacino, and Sting.

Of the many offers he received, he turned down all of them

except one—the Port Authority's free lifetime pass to the observation deck on top of the south tower. He accepted that offer because it represented who he was and what he wanted to be remembered for. Years later, he returned to the south tower, where in just 45 minutes he had captured the attention and admiration of the entire world.

When it was all over, Guy Tozzoli of the New York Port Authority interviewed Philippe. Tozzoli asked him, "What's the crucial moment?"

Philippe responded, "There's that moment when you have one foot on the building and one foot on the wire, and you have to take this foot off the building and put it on the wire." He said that at that moment, you go "into another world. And you're out there."

TRANSITION STATEMENT:

Philippe's dream would never have become a reality if he hadn't taken that step out onto the wire. Six years of preparation came down to that final crucial moment.

Do you think most people would take that step? Would you be willing to take that step? Think of Philippe's statement: "There's a moment when you have to take this foot off the building and put it on the wire." Imagine for a moment what it was like for Philippe to leave the security of that building and step on a thin wire.

The first step is the hardest.

When it comes to our relationship with God, some of us have one foot on the building and one foot on the wire right now.

God wants us to step out in faith and totally depend on him. God doesn't want us to just stand there with one foot on the building, saying we trust him. God wants us to take our foot off the edge and actually step out in faith—truly, unquestionably putting our trust in him.

APPLICATION AND SCRIPTURE:

This story reminds me of all of the stories in the Bible where people step out in faith and experience the power and stability of God. But in each story a moment arrives when God says, "Come," and they have to take that first step of faith.

In the book of Matthew, we saw Peter take this step of faith. Jesus walked on the water. Peter saw this and wanted to walk to Jesus. "'Come,' he said. Then Peter got down out of the boat, walked on the water and came toward Jesus" (Matthew 14:29).

When we take a step of faith, we experience the power of God. Peter saw Jesus walking on the water and simply asked Jesus if he could join him. Jesus said one word—"Come." In that one word, Jesus was saying, "This power is all yours if you just leave the comfort of your boat and step on the water."

That's a common theme in the Bible: Get out of your comfort zone and step out. Moses saw a poisonous snake hissing on the ground, and God said, "Want to experience the power of God? Pick it up." In faith, Moses picked up the snake by the tail, and the snake became a staff.

The children of Israel, running from Pharaoh's armies, came to the Red Sea. They were trapped. God said, "Come on in." They had to take that risky step of faith and march between the waters.

Forty years later, the children of Israel were on the eastern side of the Jordan River and God said, "Come on in—take this land." But they had to step out by faith, and when they entered the water, the waters backed up for miles while they crossed on dry land.

Those are just a few of the stories. There are many more in the Bible. And they all have one thing in common: When God said, "Come," people took a step of faith to experience that power.

What about your story? What step of faith do you need to take? What secure building do you still rest one foot on? What's the comfort zone you need to leave behind to take the first step of faith?

Maybe it's stepping away from a relationship you know is wrong. You need to step out in faith that God knows best for you—but you feel so secure in this relationship. Perhaps you have an opportunity to help someone, befriend someone, or serve God in a way that would take some sacrifice. You feel God urging you to take the step of faith, but it might take time away from your independence and fun, and it could even affect your popularity or status.

Maybe you've never even taken the step of faith to begin a relationship with God. It's quite a step. God asks us to stop doing things our way, and to put our trust in him.

The ironic fact is that even though it looks as if we're stepping from something solid to a thin wire—faith in God is actually stepping from shaky ground to a solid foundation.

But it starts with a step out of our comfort zone. It starts with a step of faith.

CLOSING

As I pray, think about this. Taking this step of faith is not about you. It's about what God wants to do in your life by his power, not yours.

Sample Prayer: *Father, this is scary. This is frightening. But I want to give you my fears and my anxiety about leaving my comfort zone of _____. Give me the strength to take a step of faith and totally depend on you.*

Sources: *To Reach The Clouds*, Philippe Petit
The Observer Magazine, Adam Higginbotham, Sunday, January 19, 2003
http://www.pbs.org/wgbh/amex/newyork/sfeature/sf_int_pop_04_04_tr_qry.html

TALK 19

TITLE: HAVING IT ALL

TOPIC: Temporary vs. Eternal

BIG IDEA: Popularity, status, good looks, and material possessions will never fulfill us. Only Christ fulfills.

SCRIPTURE:

> "But those who hope in the LORD will renew their strength. They will soar on wings like eagles; they will run and not grow weary, they will walk and not be faint." (Isaiah 40:31)

PARTICULARS:

This talk is a fictional story I wrote based on the true story of a high school student in Arizona. I heard this young man's story from a counselor at a camp where I spoke years ago. I've used the story many times to talk to kids about what they are pursuing in life.

THE STORY:

Jeremy had it all.

Let's face it. Some kids are just born with good looks, intelligence, and athletic ability. Jeremy had all this and more. Growing up, he was the most popular kid in his class in every grade. On Valentine's Day, Jeremy received the most cards. On Christmas, he could barely fit all his candy and presents in his school bag.

Jeremy always accompanied the prettiest girls to school dances. He was always surrounded by friends at the lunch table.

His ability was unmatched on the football field. In the first three games of his junior year, Jeremy caught 17 passes, scored five touchdowns, averaged 23 yards per reception, and set a school record for longest run after a catch. He intercepted a pass and scampered 88 yards for a touchdown in the season opener. Jeremy was everybody's best friend in the locker room and on the field. Everyone said hi when they passed him in the hall. Even teachers would congratulate him on a game well played. "Good game last Friday, Jeremy."

Jeremy's family wasn't rich by any means, but they always stretched to try to provide Jeremy with what he wanted. He wore the most current clothes and had more shoes than most of the girls at school. Jeremy had the latest iPod and the newest PlayStation. He always had friends over because his house was *the* place to be.

Jeremy had it all.

But Jeremy didn't realize it was all just temporary.

Jeremy was doing well in school. He wasn't going to be an astrophysicist by any means, but he got decent grades—decent enough to be on the football team, anyway. And that's all that mattered to Jeremy. As a junior, he already had scouts from five different schools keeping an eye on him. He wasn't going to have to go out and pound the doors of any colleges. They were coming to him.

As his junior year drew to a close, Jeremy was invited to a houseboat trip on Memorial Day weekend with a local church that a handful of the football players attended. The trip would last four days and three nights at Lake Powell. Jeremy didn't go to church and didn't really want to start going, but more than 100 kids would be on this trip—including Natalie Higgins, a cheerleader. That was good enough for Jeremy.

Jeremy had a great time that weekend. He didn't know many of the people going into the trip, but making friends was never difficult for Jeremy. He struck up a friendship with two other kids from his school: Blake, a senior on the varsity football team, and Josh, a soccer player. Jeremy learned that these two attended this church regularly, along with Natalie.

Each morning and evening they had what the church group called a *meeting*. Jeremy hadn't really experienced anything like it before. They started by singing a bunch of songs led by some guy with a guitar. Jeremy didn't know any of the songs, but he didn't mind listening to everyone else. Most of the kids seemed to enjoy the singing. Even Josh and Blake sang a little bit. But some kids just sat there or whispered to each other during the singing. It usually only lasted 15 or 20 minutes.

Then a kid would stand up to share what they called a *testimony*. Jeremy quickly figured out that this was just a story of the person's life and experiences with God.

After the testimony, the youth leader—a small chunky guy named Brandon—gave a little talk. Jeremy thought Brandon was pretty entertaining. He was funny and told lots of stories.

But Jeremy hadn't counted on what he was hearing. This Brandon guy was talking about the difference between temporary and eternal. He said that much of what we surround ourselves with in this life is just temporary. At first this struck Jeremy as bizarre, like some funky Confucius teaching. But something deep in Jeremy's gut told him Brandon was right.

On Saturday they all went rock jumping. A nearby cliff next to the lake started about 10 feet above the water and angled up to about 50 feet high. Some of the kids who'd been on the trip the year before ran up the cliff to jump in the water, but Brandon told them to wait until they checked it out. Two adult sponsors with diving masks swam over to the area below the cliffs and investigated the depth. In a few moments they gave the thumbs-up and the kids began jumping in. Blake told Jeremy that this spot was great because the cliff went straight down into the water for another 20 or 30 feet. The group came here every year. It was a great place to jump because the water was so deep.

Some of the kids jumped at the 10-foot mark and others at the 20. Jeremy went with Blake and Josh to the 30-foot mark and jumped in. This got quite a bit of attention. Jeremy liked that. So he decided not to waste his time with any of these smaller feats. On his second jump, he walked right up to the 50-foot mark and looked down. Everyone stopped what they were doing and watched him. He leaped from the cliff, doing a beautiful swan dive the whole way down, and barely left a splash as he entered the water. Cheers erupted as Jeremy's head popped out of the water seconds later. He gave the thumbs-up sign, and once again he was the most popular kid in the group.

Sunday night was their last night together. They sang, a girl shared her testimony, and then Brandon talked. Jeremy listened intently, because every word Brandon spoke rang true. Brandon said, "Some of us think that all this temporary stuff brings us happiness. And it does—temporarily. But what about when it's gone? Because that's the nature of temporary things. They only last a little while. The question isn't *if* the thrill will end, the question is *when* will it end."

That made Jeremy think. He definitely was satisfied with his life at the moment. Could this guy be right? Could all of this be just temporary?

Brandon went on. "Some of you might think that all the right clothes, a nice car, and a bunch of friends will make you happy. Some of you might have your life planned out ahead of you. But let me ask you this one question: What's holding it all together? What happens if all your friends, your stuff, and your future are snatched away from you tomorrow?" He paused for what seemed like an eternity. "What then?"

Jeremy sat in silence for a minute or two pondering these words. What if everything was snatched away? *What then?* Jeremy began thinking it through. He thought specifically about some of his stuff. If his house burned down, there was insurance—he could get it replaced. If he lost a friend, he had plenty of others. And it's not like he was going to lose his scholarships. Yes, it was possible to lose them, but he figured he'd just have to be sure not to do drugs or anything like that that could hinder his future.

As Jeremy continued to work this out in his mind, Brandon went on to talk about a relationship with God and how nothing could snatch that away.

Immediately after the talk, Natalie came over and sat next to him. For the next few hours they hung out together. The next morning Jeremy found Natalie again and ate breakfast with her and her friends. The two of them even rode next to each other on the bus trip home.

Jeremy finished his junior year with Natalie as his girlfriend.

On his last day of school, Jeremy was a snapshot of the perfect life. He had everything anyone could have wanted: Good looks, a beautiful girlfriend, a ton of friends, an open door to some of the best colleges in the country, and all the right toys.

Jeremy had it all.

The day after school was out there was a huge party at the river. It seemed like the whole school was there.

Some of the football players began jumping off an eight-foot rock that hung out over the river. Before long everyone was jumping. Jeremy saw the higher cliff next to the rock and knew what he had to do.

Jeremy climbed up the cliff and stood on the edge looking down about 30 feet to the shiny water's surface. He could see his reflection in the water even from 30 feet up. Everyone looked up at him as he took off his shirt. As all his friends began cheering, Jeremy dove another perfect dive into the water. But this time he wouldn't pop his head up to give a thumbs-up. Because Jeremy broke his neck the instant he hit the sandbar three feet below the surface of the water.

Exactly one year later, the snapshot of Jeremy looked a little bit different. Jeremy was paralyzed. His body was gaunt and he barely had the use of his arms. He didn't graduate with the rest of his class. He never received scholarships to any of the colleges that had been interested in him, and his circle of friends slowly drifted away to their own promising futures.

Everything had been snatched away.

Jeremy had nothing.

He was miserable, because his happiness had been dependent on circumstances. And when circumstances changed for the worse, Jeremy was no longer happy.

Fourteen months after the accident, Jeremy went to visit Brandon, the chunky youth leader from the houseboat trip. Brandon had visited Jeremy in the hospital several times and even coordinated some meals for the family during the initial tragedy. As Jeremy went through physical therapy, Brandon let him know that his door was always open if Jeremy wanted to talk. It was 14 months before Jeremy rolled through Brandon's door at the church.

Jeremy and Brandon talked for about 30 minutes. They talked about how quickly things can change. In tears, Jeremy confessed, "You were right. It was all temporary. It was all snatched away."

Brandon told him, "Yes, the temporary stuff was snatched away.

But there's something you can have that can never be snatched away. Never."

Weeping, Jeremy prayed and began a relationship with God right there in Brandon's office. He prayed, "God, I'm so sorry I thought that temporary stuff was the answer. It wasn't. I'm sorry for trying it my way. It's time I give my life to you and live it your way."

As Jeremy finished praying, he felt joyful for the first time in his life. He didn't have an ounce of that temporary happiness left, but he was overflowing with joy and purpose.

Jeremy is a counselor to this day. He is devoting his life to bringing the hope of Jesus to the hopeless, because Jeremy knows that empty road well.

TRANSITION STATEMENT:

As some of us sit here today, we realize that our happiness is dependent on circumstances.

Bottom line: When things are going well, we're happy. When things aren't going well, we're sad.

Some of us might believe that things make us happy. Some of us might have our lives planned out. But what happens if all our friends, our stuff, and our future are snatched away from us tomorrow? What then?

In the story, Jeremy was miserable, because his happiness was dependent on circumstances. And when circumstances changed for the worse, Jeremy was no longer happy.

What's the answer?

APPLICATION AND SCRIPTURE:

There is a magnificent answer for us in Isaiah 40:31:

> "But those who hope in the LORD will renew their strength. They will soar on wings like eagles; they will run and not grow weary, they will walk and not be faint."

This verse was written to Israel while they were captives in Babylon. In other words, circumstances had changed for the worse! At one time, the people of Israel had it all. They were the powerhouse of the world. All countries were in awe of Israel and their God. But then it was all taken away. Their temple was destroyed, their cities were in ruin, and the people were taken captive. They were at one of the lowest points of their history, weak and tired. They wondered if God even cared.

It's in this context that Isaiah gives them hope. The 40th chapter of Isaiah is about how God is the Creator and sustainer of all life. In verses 7 and 8, Isaiah says that the grass and flowers fade away, but the word of God lasts forever. In verses 12 and 13 Isaiah says that God holds the ocean in his hands and all nations are nothing in comparison to him. In verses 18 and 19 he says that nothing can compare to God. In verse 26 he asks the people to look at the stars and remember that God created them. Isaiah ends the chapter with some great news: He says that when we put our hope in God, the eternal, he gives us strength to endure the loss of the temporary.

Isaiah was not promising temporary happiness based on temporary things. He wasn't telling the people of Israel that they would be released from Babylon. He was giving them something much better. He was promising that they could fly above their circumstances. They were going to gain new supernatural strength to not only endure the bad, but do well in it.

Jeremy did this. He received this kind of strength from God. As a result of the supernatural strength God gives, we can soar like eagles, run and not get tired, and walk and not become weary. This is a metaphor of what happens when we pray, as Jeremy did, "God, I'm so sorry that I thought that temporary stuff was the answer. It wasn't. I'm sorry for trying it my way. It's time I give my life to you and live it your way."

Our strength is not in the temporary. It's in the eternal.

CLOSING:

Some of us need to pray that prayer right now. Pray with me.

TALK 20

TITLE: THE BRIEFCASE

TOPIC: Faith

BIG IDEA: Faith means letting go.

SCRIPTURE:

> "For although they knew God, they neither glorified him as God nor gave thanks to him, but their thinking became futile and their foolish hearts were darkened. Although they claimed to be wise, they became fools." (Romans 1:21-22)

PARTICULARS:

This parable helps kids understand what it means to truly put their trust in God—because trusting God means letting go.

THE STORY:

Larry had a choice to make: the briefcase, or the hand reaching to save him. As he hung on the edge of the cliff, it became crystal clear that he couldn't have both.

Three days before, Larry had decided to retire from his life of crime. He wasn't a violent criminal, and he never took from someone who didn't deserve it—or so he told himself. Larry was a regular Robin Hood. He stole from the rich, and gave to—well—himself. So he really only lived half of Robin Hood's legacy—the stealing half!

Larry made his decision to retire shortly after he received a phone call from Andy on a rainy Tuesday morning. Andy was an information magnet. Larry had never seen him outside his beach condo, where he spent all his time staring at three 21-inch screens hooked up to his network of computers. Andy was pipelined to a wealth of information about trading, commerce, gambling, and "business transactions," as he called them.

Andy had provided Larry with most of the intel behind his heists. Andy could get it all: Blueprints, floor plans, schematics—you name it. Some of his information was so detailed that the only thing left to do was pull up to a building, punch a code in an access panel, disappear inside for five minutes, and walk out a millionaire.

But that took risk. Risk paid better than intel. Larry was willing to take that risk. That's why Larry made 80 percent and Andy made 20 percent.

Andy never had to leave his house.

When Larry arrived at Andy's that rainy Tuesday morning, he had no idea what to expect. Andy usually had three or four jobs on hand. He liked Larry, so he usually gave Larry his pick. The jobs ranged from safety deposit box scams to ripping off major corporations.

Andy let Larry in the front door. Andy didn't waste any time. "I've got your 401k right here," he said, tapping the manila folder in his hand with his forefinger.

"My 401k?"

"Yeah," Andy smiled, keeping Larry in suspense. "Your 401k. Your retirement job. Do this one last job, and you can retire."

Larry raised an eyebrow. "How much?"

"Seven figures. But this one is so sweet, my cut is 30 percent."

Larry reached for the folder, but Andy pulled it back out of reach. "Thirty percent?"

Larry paused for a second. "I have to see the details first."

Andy was used to this with Larry. Andy would provide Larry with some of the vague details—no names or addresses, but enough details to give him a basic idea of the difficulty of the job. The bottom line was always highlighted in yellow. As Larry opened this folder, his eyes immediately zeroed in on the figure written in yellow. It was $14,500,000. Larry quickly figured the percentage in his head. That meant that his 70 percent would still be more than $10 million.

Larry read the overview in less than 30 seconds and agreed on the percentage. Andy handed him a thicker manila folder with all the details. Larry reviewed the material for the next 20 minutes, asking questions, clarifying some of the numbers.

This job would be a little different from most he'd done. It was only three days away. That wasn't a lot of time to plan. He'd have to fly into Atlanta and drive north a few hours. The job was in a hotel resort just outside Chattanooga, of all places. He'd be relying on information from an employee. Larry didn't like relying on people. He made an exception for Andy, but that was it. He didn't trust many people, and he sure wasn't excited about trusting some $30,000-a-year night-shift manager.

But every other detail looked good to Larry—and Andy had vouched for this guy. Andy didn't usually vouch for someone unless they were like family to Andy. Not to mention that this guy's percentage was already considered in Andy's percentage.

Larry sat back and thought about it for a minute. Ten million dollars plus was a lot of money. He could finally retire. The dotcoms had killed his retirement a decade before. Since then he'd been living from job to job—although his lifestyle wasn't exactly frugal.

Larry agreed. He finalized the details with Andy and went on his way.

Three days later Larry landed in Atlanta. He got into his rental car, a big Lincoln, and drove north.

Larry didn't know how fast he'd have to drive when he returned on the same roads that night, so he paid close attention to the curves and cross streets. He had to cross some mountains. He paused on occasion as the cars in front of him pulled off to various vista points to take a look at the gorgeous views. Some of the drop-offs were amazing—straight down, literally thousands of feet.

Larry checked into the resort around 7 p.m.—he waited until the new manager's shift began. He paid in cash and went up to his room.

The room was nice. It had a marble entry with a chandelier. The enormous bathroom was to the left. Larry peeked in, noticing the beautiful sunken tub, the cherry vanity and chair. The main part of the room was carpeted, with a large cherry desk in the corner and a plush king bed along the left wall.

Larry settled into the room and prepared for what he'd be doing in two hours.

At 9:30 on the nose Larry exited his room and used the keycard the manager had provided to enter room 2112 across the hall.

Larry breathed a sigh of relief when the room was empty. He went to the closet and opened up the large doors. The safe was in the left wall. Larry quickly punched in the code—another gift from the manager—and almost shouted in triumph when the latch opened.

The only item in the safe was a large briefcase.

Larry slid it out and picked it up, shifting his weight to lift it. Andy had warned him it would weigh almost 50 pounds because of what was inside it. Larry smiled as he felt the weight of the case.

One hour later Larry drove the same mountain roads heading back to Atlanta, but with his eyes on the rearview mirror. As Larry peeked back at the following headlights, he thought it was too much of a coincidence. A car had made the last three turns with Larry and had driven behind him for the last 30 minutes. Larry knew that when it came to this kind of money, even the most trusted sources couldn't be trusted. He feared that the hotel manager had made a deal with others for a higher percentage.

But Larry wasn't going to waste time thinking about the "who" right now. He needed to lose this tail so he could make his escape. He had backup flight plans under another passport, and it looked like those were the ones he was going to be using.

Larry mashed the pedal to the floor of the Lincoln, navigating the turns with precision, accelerating out of each turn. To Larry's surprise, the vehicle behind him didn't pursue him. Traveling up to 80 miles per hour, depending on the curves, Larry put a quarter mile of distance between himself and the headlights in no time.

As Larry approached a curve he gave his rearview mirror one last check. He thought he could see the lights three curves back. It was hard to see because they'd disappear behind a curve, then reappear again. It took him several seconds to get a bearing on where the car was.

That's probably why he miscalculated the curve in front of him. When he took his eyes off the mirror and looked forward again, he noticed he'd drifted into the lane of oncoming traffic. The headlights of a truck headed right toward him. A horn blared. Reflexively, he steered hard to the right—a little too hard. His right wheels dropped off the shoulder.

He cut the wheel hard to the left, trying to get his wheels back on the road. But they were sliding through dirt and gravel and weren't grabbing onto anything. It happened so fast that Larry didn't realize how far he'd overcorrected to the left, because when the wheels finally did hit pavement and grab, the Lincoln veered hard to the left and flipped three times in the air before it even hit the ground. Finally, it hit the guardrail.

The side of the Lincoln hit so hard it looked as if it would take the guardrail down with it. But when the dust settled, the car, now on its side dangling off the cliff, miraculously held on to a piece of torn metal from the guardrail.

When the gold Toyota Camry pulled up to the accident, the Lincoln was barely visible over the edge of the cliff. From one angle it looked as if it were levitating on its side, ready to drop at any second. A young man wearing a Marine Corps sweatshirt ran from the Camry toward the broken guardrail. His wife followed. Looking down the cliff, he could see into the cab of the car where Larry was sitting, belted into the driver's seat, a dazed expression on his face, right hand outstretched and holding desperately to a briefcase.

The car had broken one of the guardrail posts completely in half. The posts at the front and the rear of the car were intact; they held the torn metal that was somehow preventing the huge luxury car from falling.

The car sat sideways. Larry slowly turned his head to look out the right passenger window. He could see about 1,000 feet straight down.

Without hesitation the Marine grabbed the nub of the broken guardrail post sticking out of the ground with one arm. Reaching down with his other arm, he offered his hand to Larry.

Larry blinked twice and looked at the Marine's outstretched hand. The window was broken and the hand was easily within reach. Larry tried to lift the briefcase with his right hand—but he couldn't lift it. His shoulder felt as if it were being pulled out of its socket. He couldn't lift that kind of weight, so the briefcase just hung there in his hand, swinging like a pendulum.

Larry started to reach for the man's hand with his left arm, but realized it would do no good. He was belted in. If he unbelted himself, his body would drop to the right side of the car. He adjusted his body to look for the seat-belt button. When Larry's body turned, the car shifted ever so slightly. The metal of the guardrail groaned.

The Marine yelled, "Grab my hand!"

Larry reached his left arm out to the Marine, and the Marine grabbed it with a powerful grip. Larry felt the car shift once again.

"What are you doing?!" the Marine yelled again. "Take off your seat-belt and give me your other hand! I don't think this fence thing is going to hold!"

Larry's arms were stretched in two different directions. His left arm stretched up the cliff, in the grip of the Marine. His right arm still stretched down, barely holding the weight of the heavy briefcase. Larry tried to see if he could lift his right arm to the seat-belt button without dropping the briefcase. It couldn't be done. The briefcase was way too heavy for his weakened shoulder, and it was impossible to get to the seat-belt button with the briefcase in his hand. The only way he could release the seat-belt button was to let go of the briefcase.

The Marine yelled once again, puzzled by Larry's hesitancy. "Undo your seat-belt! What are you doing?!"

Larry looked in the Marine's eyes. "My briefcase. I need my briefcase."

"Forget your briefcase, you idiot! Let go of it and undo your seat-belt!"

Larry looked down at his briefcase again and tried to lift it. He couldn't move it in the slightest. He could barely keep his grip on the handle. But he didn't allow himself to lose the grip. That briefcase was his retirement.

Larry looked at the Marine and repeated the same words slowly. "I need my briefcase!"

The guardrail groaned again and the car seemed to adjust itself and slip about an inch.

The Marine curled his lip. "Listen to me, and listen to me good. It's my hand, or the briefcase! Because this car is going down. My hand is here for you, but you've got to let go of the briefcase."

Larry shut his eyes and exhaled. Then he looked at the Marine and repeated himself one more time. "I need my briefcase."

The Marine didn't budge. "Let go of the briefcase and undo your seat-belt, you fool!"

Larry calculated in his head again. "Let go of my arm for a second."

"What?" the Marine questioned.

"Let go of my arm for just a second!" Larry pulled on his left arm and the Marine let go. Larry had it figured out. He pushed with his feet to hold his body against the seat. He would reach over with his left hand and undo the seat-belt, then reach back for the guy's hand.

"Let go of the briefcase," the Marine pleaded one last time.

Larry shot a stare at the Marine as he reached his left arm down toward his seat-belt release. "I've got time. Just let me..."

There was a loud pop. The car, Larry, and the briefcase fell into the darkness without a sound.

TRANSITION STATEMENT:

Larry had a choice. An outstretched hand, or the briefcase. The only way to free himself was to let go.

Larry couldn't let go.

I've sometimes heard people ask the question, "Why would a loving God send people to hell?"

The Bible says that God doesn't want anyone to perish. No one! He's literally got his arms stretched out to us, offering eternal life with him.

There's one requirement: *Let go.*

That's what faith in God means: Letting go of our way and trusting God's way. And that's the catch for so many of us. We aren't willing to let go. We aren't willing to accept the hand offered to us, because we can't let go of what we're holding on to.

APPLICATION AND SCRIPTURE:

God doesn't send people to hell—they choose it.

This might sound foreign to you. It's not politically correct, but it's true. In the Bible, the apostle Paul talks about people who have a choice—those who can see God reaching out to them—but who reject his loving arms because they choose to invent their own gods; gods that promise to fulfill their selfish dreams.

> "For although they knew God, they neither glorified him as God nor gave thanks to him, but their thinking became futile and their foolish hearts were darkened. Although they claimed to be wise, they became fools." (Romans 1:21-22)

Paul keeps using a phrase over and over again:

> "Therefore God gave them over in the sinful desires of their hearts to sexual impurity for the degrading of their bodies with one another."
> (Romans 1:24)

"Because of this, God gave them over
to shameful lusts..." (Romans 1:26)

"...God gave them over to a depraved mind..."
(Romans 1:28)

What Paul meant by "God gave them over..." could be translated, "If you decide to choose life without me, I'm not going to force you to choose me. You can go your own way, and I'll leave you alone. It's your choice."

And the result of that choice is a life without God, which the Bible calls *hell*—an eternal life without God's grace, God's love, God's presence, and God's protection.

Author C.S. Lewis puts it this way: "The doors of Hell are locked from the inside."

The young Marine didn't grab Larry and force the briefcase out of his hand. It was up to Larry to let go and accept the help.

CLOSING:

Larry had a choice. In reality, *you* have a choice. You can either hold on to your own way—a way that leads to life without God. Or you can let go and take God's outstretched hand.

It's your choice. And you can make it right now.

Let's pray right now. Some of you might want to make that choice to let go and reach for God.

TALK 21

TITLE: HARD-LEARNED LESSONS

TOPIC: Fulfillment

BIG IDEA: Jesus is the only thing that can fill our emptiness.

SCRIPTURE:

> "Repent, then, and turn to God, so that your sins may be wiped out, that times of refreshing may come from the Lord…" (Acts 3:19)

PARTICULARS:

This is the true story of a friend of mine. I changed the names and some small details for anonymity. It was amazing to see Christ change this young man's life. His story is an inspiration.

THE STORY:

Stewart never wanted to be an alcoholic. He never woke up one morning and decided he wanted to be a drug addict and get thrown in jail. He just wanted to be happy. And he figured that the best way to achieve this was to do things *his* way.

It probably started when he was 13—that's the *first* time he got in trouble with the law. Stewart waited until his dad fell asleep and then sneaked into his garage, pulling the release switch for the automatic garage door and silently lifting the door manually. Five minutes later he was pushing his car silently down the street so his father didn't hear it start up in front of the house.

Stewart was glad his father's Dodge was an automatic. It wasn't much harder to drive than the Indy Racers he drove at Green Acres Mini-Golf Land—gas and brake. He picked up his 13-year-old girl-friend at her house, and the two of them sped off down the street. Two streets actually—because that's the farthest they got before Stewart cornered so hard he lost control, running the car up on someone's lawn, hitting one of those big green electrical boxes, and knocking out the power for several blocks.

When Stewart's dad got the phone call from the police station, he told them to hold him overnight. "Maybe that will teach him a lesson," he said.

It didn't.

By the time Stewart was 14 he got in trouble at school almost every day. He didn't see himself as a troublemaker—he just lived his life doing whatever he wanted to do. He figured that was the key to being happy. If he wanted to do something, he did it. If it looked good to him, he'd take it.

That's probably why he started drinking at 14.

As a freshman in high school, Stewart found himself at a party after every soccer game. That's what the soccer players did. They found a house where the parents weren't home, consumed large amounts of alcohol, and woke up the next day with a headache, wondering what had happened the night before.

This got old pretty fast. So Stewart tried something new. Three of his buddies smoked a lot of weed. Stewart didn't want to be a pothead, but he thought marijuana was at least worth a try.

Stewart loved it at first. Everyone's jokes were funnier. The stress of school, home, and soccer were gone—for an hour or two, anyway. As a matter of fact, Stewart liked everything about smoking bud, except that the more he smoked it, the more he wanted.

Stewart developed a habit by 16, and he needed money to pay for it. Between school and soccer practice, he didn't really have time for a job (and didn't want a job, for that matter), so money was hard to come by.

His dad had stopped giving him allowance long ago, and Stewart consumed way too much weed to get away with bumming off his friends every time. Besides, Stewart didn't want to be a free-loader.

One night when he and his buddies ran out of pot, they met up with a "friend of a friend" who offered them a good deal.

Next thing they knew, Stewart and his friends were breaking into a garage and ripping off expensive auto repair tools. This "friend" gave them a good price for the tools—enough to party for a week.

Stewart was amazed by how simple it was. Steal, sell—party all week. That's how he began his career of breaking and entering.

By age 17 Stewart had been busted by the cops many times. A few DUIs, a couple of small burglaries, but the charges never stuck—nothing that scared him enough to get him to stop.

But when Stewart was 17, something else happened. He met a girl at school unlike any other girl he'd ever met. Her name was Tabitha, and she sat next to Stewart in Spanish II. Tabitha was a beautiful brunette with smooth skin and sincere blue eyes. She also played soccer, but she never went to the parties afterward. Stewart kept inviting her, but she wasn't interested. One day he asked her why she never wanted to go to any of the parties, and she told him. It was because she was usually at her church youth group. And Tabitha invited Stewart right then to go to church with her.

Stewart laughed out loud. "Sorry, I'm not into church."

But she told him about an upcoming snow-skiing weekend— three days in a cabin with her church youth group. They'd ski all day Saturday and hang out in the ski lodge. It sounded pretty fun— all except the church part.

But Stewart couldn't say no to those blue eyes and skiing, so he signed up for the trip.

Imagine his surprise when he arrived at the trip to find 80-plus kids in a ski lodge for the weekend with no alcohol and no drugs. He figured this was going to be one of the lamest weekends he'd spent in years.

But it wasn't.

Stewart couldn't remember the last time he'd had so much fun. The people were nice, the skiing was fun, and some of Tabitha's friends were as pretty as she was. No complaints.

Each night the church group had a "meeting," as they called it. At this meeting they sang songs (which didn't particularly interest Stewart), and this one guy spoke about a life with Christ. He talked about how Christ could fill our emptiness in life. Stewart hadn't been to church more than twice in his whole life, but he didn't have anything against God. He just figured he'd go his own way and let God go his. No worries. It had worked so far.

When Stewart got home from the weekend, nothing changed. As a matter of fact, he even got a few chances to party that week. But he noticed something; When the partying was over and he found himself back in his bedroom, in bed; staring at the ceiling—he felt as if something was missing.

This was crazy, if you really think about it. Stewart had lived his whole life doing whatever he wanted to do. If he wanted something, he took it. If he felt like doing something, he did it. He'd tried to fill every desire he ever had.

But here he was, lying in bed, staring at the ceiling, wondering, "What now?"

He was empty.

That guy at the church weekend was right. He felt a certain emptiness.

Stewart didn't think Christ was necessarily the answer, but he was definitely feeling that emptiness. He needed to try to fill it.

When the next Friday rolled around, Stewart got completely wasted. He drove his mom's truck to a party at someone's house he didn't even know. He drank almost an entire bottle of vodka, smoked all the bud in his pocket, and then tried something completely new—someone offered him a hit of acid. Stewart had heard about acid, but he figured, *Why not?* So he dropped acid.

This was a whole new ball game. It was like nothing he'd experienced before. He just sat there on this stranger's couch and watched the room slowly expand and contract as if it were breathing. He sat on the couch watching the room breathe for the next two hours. And then he took off with his friends, doing things he didn't even remember.

Around 2:30 in the morning, someone in his mom's apartment complex saw Stewart squeal into the parking lot and park his mom's truck sideways across two parking spots. Stewart got out of the truck, stumbled to the rear of the vehicle, lay down on the asphalt, rolled underneath the car, and went to sleep.

The neighbor called the police.

Stewart woke up when two policemen dragged him from underneath the truck. When he saw the policeman's face, it began to grow hair out of its eyeballs, and the teeth turned into fangs. Stewart's last memory of the evening was swinging at the hairy creature in the police uniform. Then he passed out.

When Stewart woke up in the morning he had 13 counts against him—three of them felony charges. This time, Stewart wasn't going to get away with anything. The only thing in his favor was the fact that he was not yet 18.

Stewart went to Juvenile Hall.

Stewart began his four-month detox at Juvenile Hall by getting jumped by three guys. Stewart was a big guy—one of the biggest there—so the other big guys had to let him know who was in charge quickly.

Getting beaten up a few times didn't bother him. Stewart was fighting other fights right now. His body was crying out for things that weren't available in Juvenile Hall. To make matters worse, every time Stewart lay down and looked up at the ceiling—it came back. The emptiness.

There isn't a lot to do in Juvenile Hall. So Stewart spent a lot of time thinking. He'd lived his life trying to achieve happiness by doing whatever he wanted. Unfortunately, doing whatever he wanted seemed to be a recipe for misery. Stewart was anything but fulfilled. He knew there had to be something else out there.

That's when he noticed the Bible on the shelf.

Stewart had never been much of a reader, but it only took three days of staring at the walls before he finally thought he'd give the Bible a try. For the next four months, he read the whole thing from cover to cover. He didn't understand a lot of the stuff near the beginning, but he understood one thing really clearly: A bunch of the people in the Bible kept letting God down by doing things their own way instead of God's way. Stewart knew that lifestyle well. He'd lived his whole life that way. But God loved these people so much that he decided to come down to earth himself in the form of a human named Jesus. And people decided to reject him as Jesus, too. They killed him on a cross, and God didn't even fight back.

The Bible was clear. If Stewart wanted a relationship with God, he just had to put his faith in God. Jesus was willing to pay for all the bad stuff he'd done. It was paid for by Jesus on that cross. All he needed to do was put his trust in God. That didn't mean just saying, "I believe," and going back to his old ways. The Bible was pretty clear about that. God didn't take fakes. But for those who truly believed in him—God took them in.

The week Stewart got out of Juvenile Hall, he received a phone call. It was Tabitha.

"Do you want to go to church with me this Sunday?"

Stewart didn't even hesitate. "What time can you pick me up?" He wouldn't be driving for a while now.

That Sunday, not three days after Stewart got out of Juvenile Hall, the preacher talked about how so many of us try to live life our way instead of God's way. Stewart hung on every word. At the end of the message, the pastor gave an opportunity for people to give their lives to Jesus. Right there, in the third row of this small church, Stewart prayed and gave his life to Jesus. He said, "God, you know what a mess my life is. I've done everything I wanted and I'm empty. I think I need to give your way a try."

TRANSITION STATEMENT:

Many of us haven't tried the things that Stewart tried, but we might relate to the feeling he had when he went to bed at night and felt empty.

Anyone who's tried to live life their own way knows what a lonely and miserable life it can be. For Stewart, it took hitting rock bottom to realize this. It took jail time to help him realize he needed God.

APPLICATION AND SCRIPTURE:

Don't wait until you hit bottom. You can experience fulfillment now.

We can make the same choice Stewart eventually made. We can stop going our own way, turn around, and go God's way. The Bible calls this act *repenting*. It basically means doing a 180 and going God's way instead of our own.

The book of Acts says, "Repent, then, and turn to God, so that your sins may be wiped out, that times of refreshing may come from the Lord..." (Acts 3:19)

CLOSING:

Some of us need to make that decision now. Let's bow our heads and close our eyes, thinking about ourselves, not the people sitting around us.

Some of us might relate to Stewart simply because we've felt the emptiness of doing things our own way rather than God's way. But God offers something so much better. God offers fulfillment and refreshment in a relationship with him. And that's something no one can ever take away from you.

So as you sit there right now with your eyes closed and your head bowed, I ask you this question: Are you ready for a change? Because Acts 3:19 says that you can do that right now, turning to God, and your sins will be wiped away. You can tell God right now, "Forgive me for my past; I give you my future."

You can make the same decision Stewart did. Stewart is now a firefighter living with his wife and two kids on the outskirts of Sacramento, California. And now he volunteers at his church youth group, talking to kids about the decisions they're making each day. But most importantly, when Stewart goes to bed each night, he isn't empty. Stewart has a relationship with the God who created him. This relationship is through faith in Jesus Christ.

Some of you need to make that decision right now. If you do, pray with me.

TALK 22
TITLE: STEPPING STONES

TOPIC: Evidence That Demands a Choice

BIG IDEA: Faith isn't something we have to stir up, but an objective decision to either accept or reject Christ.

SCRIPTURE:

> "And without faith it is impossible to please God, because anyone who comes to him must believe that he exists and that he rewards those who earnestly seek him." (Hebrews 11:6)

PARTICULARS:

This true story is much more intellectual than the others. It's better suited for an academic crowd, philosophical thinkers, mature high school kids, or college students.

THE STORY:

The love story of Sheldon and Davy was unique. Unique because they didn't want their marriage to grow apart as they'd seen so many marriages do. So the two of them decided to do something about it.

Sheldon Vanauken fell in love with a beautiful woman named Davy. When they married, they devised a plan to protect their marriage—an interesting idea they called "the shining barrier."

They believed this shining barrier would protect them from the wedge that drove apart so many marriages. They didn't want their relationship to slowly drift apart. So Sheldon and Davy made a commitment not to let that happen to them. In their minds, the rules of the shining barrier would help them achieve this.

One of the rules was that if one person learned some knowledge or a skill, then they'd both learn it. For example, if one person wanted to study Shakespeare, they'd both learn Shakespeare. If one person decided to learn French, they'd both learn French. If one person decided to build a boat, they'd build the boat together and sail around the world.

This might sound extreme to many of us, but to this young couple it was love. They even decided not to have children because they thought that could pull them apart.

This true love story is told in Sheldon's book *A Severe Mercy*.

But then it happened.

A crack developed in the shining barrier. When they went to Oxford to study at the university, they met a man by the name of C.S. Lewis. (You might know that name because C.S. Lewis is the author of the Chronicles of Narnia series.) Through their contact with C.S. Lewis, Davy became a Christian. Think about the ramifications of this decision when considering Sheldon and Davy's "shining barrier." If one became a Christian, they must both become Christians.

Sheldon was furious.

He didn't understand how anyone in her right mind could think that the reality of Christ was true. He felt he could never make the leap intellectually to accept Christ's teachings. But most of all, Sheldon was angry that the shining barrier had been penetrated.

It got worse. For Sheldon, the breaking of the shining barrier was bad enough, but then the love of his life was totally ripped away. Davy died. (I'm not giving this away if you're going to read the book, because you find out in the very first chapter.)

He was devastated.

Sheldon and C.S. Lewis began corresponding through letters. In these letters Sheldon vented his anger and bitterness, but he also asked questions. C.S. Lewis knew these questions well. He wrote back with incredible insight, having suffered the same loss years prior. When C.S. Lewis' wife Joy died of cancer, his rock-solid faith in Christ was sideswiped, and he experienced doubt for the first time in his life. Lewis said, "Nothing will shake a man out of his merely notional beliefs. He has to be knocked silly before he comes to his senses. Only torture will bring out the truth. Only under torture does he discover it himself" (C.S. Lewis, *A Grief Observed*).

Sheldon's questions led to a search for truth, a quest for meaning. Sheldon described this search as hopping upstream on stepping stones. Each stone was a piece of evidence to consider and its solidity had to be considered carefully before taking that step.

Sheldon saw specific stones he was forced to consider. The first was Christ's statements about himself. Christ did something amazing that couldn't be ignored—he claimed he was God.

Sheldon couldn't bypass this stepping stone. He couldn't ignore it. Because once Christ said it, it only allowed three possibilities:

1. Christ was a liar.
2. Christ was a lunatic.
3. Christ was Lord, just as he said.

Lewis and Sheldon discussed these three possibilities. Why would Christ lie? He could've lied to save himself from death, but he didn't. Why would he die for a lie? And how could someone so wise be a lunatic? It didn't take much evaluation to realize the absurdity of that claim.

The evidence was overwhelming.

The stone was hard to ignore, and impossible to bypass.

Another stepping stone was Christ's disciples. They all testified to the resurrection, and most died martyrs' deaths.

Sheldon looked at more steps. He investigated the miracles Christ performed, particularly the resurrection. He began to look at what historians of that time had said about Christ. He examined the evidence.

This led Sheldon to examine his own need for forgiveness and the pain in his own life. That was something he couldn't deny.

So many stones, each one requiring a step.

He said that as he stood in the middle of the metaphorical river looking at the next stepping stone, he almost concluded that he couldn't take that leap of faith, even though the evidence was overwhelming.

But then he realized he was stuck.

Sheldon turned around and looked behind him. Behind him was a huge chasm of nothingness. He had to make a choice.

That's when he realized that his choice was not to *accept* Christ as the reality and objective truth. In fact, the evidence was so overwhelming that the choice was really whether or not he was going to *reject* all he'd seen. His choice was really whether or not he was going to pretend that the stepping stones *weren't there*.

Sheldon couldn't come to the place of rejecting all he'd seen. So he accepted the fact that Jesus Christ really was God, and that he really wanted a relationship with him.

Sheldon Vanauken became a Christian.

He'd be able to share that with Davy after all.

TRANSITION STATEMENT:

I don't know where you are in your faith today. Maybe you've never even ventured up this metaphorical stream Sheldon did. Many have. And most people who do have to come to a decision. Not the decision many might think—*do I accept Christ?* No, the people who go down this road need to come to the decision—*do I reject Christ?*

I ask you that. Are you ready to *reject* Christ today?

Because faith isn't just saying, "I believe in Jesus." Anyone who wants to put his faith in God must be willing to put his trust in him and walk upon the stepping stone of evidence.

APPLICATION AND SCRIPTURE:

Hebrews 11 defines faith. In verse 6 the writer says:

> "And without faith it is impossible to please God, because anyone who comes to him must believe that he exists and that he rewards those who earnestly seek him." (Hebrews 11:6)

God is not something we have to invent or stir up in our minds. God exists whether we believe in him or not. Our faith begins when we decide not to reject God.

I'm talking to two types of people today. Some of you say, "I believe in Christ." And some of you say, "I don't believe in Christ." Some might think there's a third group, a group that says, "I don't care." But remember, if someone chooses *not* to respond to Christ, if someone chooses to ignore Christ and his claims, he chooses to reject him.

So to both groups—those who accept his claims and those who reject his claims—I ask these questions:

How do you know what you believe?

Have you really looked at the evidence to be able to say, "Wow, Christ really *is* who he said he was!" or "Wow, Christ was a fraud. He was a liar and just fooled people."

I challenge you to look at the evidence of Christ. Look at his teachings in the Gospels. Look at the evidence of the resurrection; the life, death, and writings of the disciples; the growth of the early church. Go to the library and look up books about this person Christ who walked on the earth claiming he was God—dying for it, in fact. (And if you do want to investigate, let me know—I can provide trustworthy resources, too.)

But then I challenge you to do something much more difficult. Look inside yourself. Look at your need for Christ's saving love. Maybe as you look into your own life, you'll find a search for meaning and purpose—a search that has come up empty with the things of this world.

CLOSING:

I trust that if you're here today and you've never accepted Jesus Christ—if you've never made that leap—you'll discover there's no better time than now. You can turn from rejecting and you can say, "I need to accept the reality of the truth of Jesus Christ in my life today."

Let's pray. And some of you can pray that prayer right now.

TALK 23
TITLE: BLAMING GOD

TOPIC: Response to Tragedy

BIG IDEA: When people face tragedy, they usually have one of two reactions. They blame God, or they turn to God for help.

SCRIPTURE:

> "His wife said to him, 'Are you still maintaining your integrity? Curse God and die!' He replied, 'You are talking like a foolish woman. Shall we accept good from God, and not trouble?' In all this, Job did not sin in what he said." (Job 2:9-10)

PARTICULARS:

This fictional story is based on the life story of a good friend of mine who ended up being one of my youth ministry volunteers years ago. I've heard her share her story with kids many times. Her testimony always reaches out to the huge number of kids who are experiencing life's hurt.

THE STORY:

As Lisa sat at the hospital bed holding her father's hand, she knew this was it. This was the last time she was going to see him. She also knew she couldn't go through this alone.

Lisa was Daddy's girl. She always had been. She grew up the youngest of three. Her older sister and brother were only a year apart; then there was a four-year gap before Lisa.

Lisa was spoiled rotten.

In elementary school Lisa was constantly in trouble. Not big trouble by any means; let's just say she knew her way to the principal's office. But Daddy never punished Lisa much. He would quickly correct her when she acted out, then smother her with love as if nothing had happened. Lisa loved her daddy.

Lisa's family went to church together every Sunday. Lisa wasn't really sure why, but she didn't mind. She got to dress up in cute dresses and sit with her dad. Dad was so busy during the week, and church was one time Lisa got to hang out with him for hours. She didn't care if it was in a pew listening to some guy talking about God. She didn't really listen anyway. She just drew pictures and showed them to Daddy.

Family time was important in Lisa's family. Friday nights usually meant playing board games together or popping popcorn and watching a movie. No matter what pressures seemed to be hitting Lisa's family at the time, they were all pushed aside temporarily on Friday night by fun.

As Lisa went into junior high, she found herself running with a rebellious crowd. At only 12, Lisa was kissing boyfriends on Saturday nights at the skating rink and spending endless hours online chatting with cute guys across the country. Lisa never favored cyberfriends over real people. She didn't discriminate—she was happy to get into trouble with anyone.

It was at this time that Lisa and her mother began fighting. At first it was just occasionally. Then it grew to be a daily occurrence, as Lisa learned the art of backtalk, gleaning the skills from some of her unruly friends. But Lisa was smart. She toned it down whenever her father came home. She never let *him* catch her mouthing off to Mom. Besides, things were never as intense when Dad was there. Any disagreements between Mom and Lisa disappeared when the board games came out on Friday night.

By high school, Lisa was partying pretty hard. She always managed to spend the night at a friend's house or come in after her parents were asleep, evading detection of her intoxicated state.

Lisa's drinking led to a little bit of pot smoking. She didn't become an addict, but she definitely didn't turn down a free hit or two at parties.

Needless to say, she never attended church anymore. She was usually sleeping or hung over on Sunday mornings. The last thing she wanted to do was drag herself to what she considered the most boring hour of the week.

At 18 Lisa immediately moved out of the house. She couldn't handle being under the same roof as Mom anymore, but she met Dad once a week for lunch. His office was close to her school, and it was easy for them to connect on Wednesdays.

Lisa loved these times, especially since she moved out. That was the one negative of moving away. She missed her dad.

Occasionally her dad invited her to church with them. Lisa usually declined. She liked time with her dad but opted to spend it somewhere else, such as their midweek lunches. Dad never pushed, but he didn't stop inviting, either.

In Lisa's second year of college, her friend Christine invited her to a large concert event at a local church. Christine was Lisa's closest college friend. But Christine had always made God and church a priority, and Lisa hadn't. Christine occasionally invited Lisa to church or church activities, and Lisa usually declined. But on this particular Saturday night Lisa had nothing else to do, and the thought of hanging out with her friend at a concert sounded fun.

Three bands played that night in the outdoor arena. Lisa really enjoyed the music, but began eyeing the exits when they introduced a speaker. But she forgot about leaving once the speaker began. He was captivating and funny, and his words hit Lisa right where she lived.

The speaker proposed, "Maybe you've been pushing God away your whole life. Maybe you've even come up with some logical-sounding reasons why you don't want to believe in him or acknowledge him. Guess what? That doesn't stop God from loving you. God will wait you out. And when you're ready, he'll be there."

Lisa shifted in her seat a little bit. Personally, she didn't have a problem with God. But she definitely didn't want to think too much about it, because she knew if she did, she might have to start changing some things. And truthfully, she liked her life the way it was right now.

The speaker continued. "Some of you are trying to get through this world alone. But you're not alone. You have a father up in heaven who wants a relationship with you. And whatever you're going through, he'll be there. It's your choice. You can go through life with God, or you can go it alone."

Lisa didn't know how prophetic the speaker's words were for her own life, because the next week she got a phone call from her mother. She was crying. "Lisa, I don't know how to tell you this, so I'll just say it. Your father and I just got back from the hospital..." Lisa held her breath as her mother finished, "...your father has pancreatic cancer."

Lisa drove home immediately. The whole family was there. They spent hours crying together, before Dad finally said "enough" and broke out the board games.

The cancer took Dad in just three months. On his last night, Lisa sped to the hospital to sit by his side. The doctors predicted he wouldn't make it through the night. As Lisa held her father's hand and watched him sleep, she became incredibly frightened. She'd never even fathomed what it would be like to live life without him. She couldn't picture life without her daddy.

Lisa began trembling. She'd never felt so hopeless in all her life—so hopeless, in fact, that she did something she hadn't done in a long time. She prayed.

Alone in the hospital room, with her dad resting quietly beside her, Lisa looked up at the ceiling and began talking to God. "God? I don't know if you really remember me—it's been a while since I've been to church. I don't know if that concert counts."

She wiped her tears on her sleeve. "I don't even know why I'm talking to you. I guess I should be mad at you, but I'm not." Lisa looked at her father lying there peacefully. His heart rate was steady for the moment. She looked up to the ceiling again. "I don't think I can do this alone."

Lisa's sister walked into the room. She'd had a little further to drive across town. The two of them sat by his bedside, soon to be joined by their brother and their mom. Two hours later, Lisa's dad passed away.

Christine sat with Lisa and her family at the funeral. She was surprised at how well Lisa was handling the whole thing.

When the funeral was over Lisa pulled Christine aside. "I want you to pick me up for church this Sunday."

Christine couldn't believe what she was hearing. But she nodded and quickly told Lisa the time and place she'd pick her up.

Lisa saw the surprised look on Christine's face. "What—did ya think I'd never come around?"

Christine smiled. "No, it's not that. I guess I'm just glad that through all this you're still considering church."

Lisa sighed. "I'll be honest with you. I'm not excited about church. But I can either go through this with God, or go it alone. And frankly, I don't want to do this alone."

Lisa started attending church with Christine and soon committed her life to following Christ. She even began working with kids in the church and trying to help them make better choices in their lives.

To this day if you meet Lisa, she'll tell you that it was only through her father's death that she finally realized how much she needed God. She misses her daddy, but she looks forward to seeing him again someday soon.

TRANSITION STATEMENT:

When people face tragedy, they usually have one of two reactions. They blame God, or they turn to God for help.

Lisa could have blamed God, but she was honest with herself and realized that she needed him.

APPLICATION AND SCRIPTURE:

Lisa's reaction reminds us of the reactions of Job, compared to his wife's, in the Bible. Notice how one blamed God, and the other turned to God for help.

> "His wife said to him, 'Are you still maintaining your integrity? Curse God and die!' He replied, 'You are talking like a foolish woman. Shall we accept good from God, and not trouble?' In all this, Job did not sin in what he said." (Job 2:9-10)

In the Bible, the book of Job is a study in how people respond to loss, pain, and suffering. Job lost everything—his wealth, his health, his standing in the community, and his seven children. Job's wife experienced the same suffering and had to comfort a husband who was in excruciating pain.

But notice the two responses.

Job's wife blamed God. She was angry and said, "Curse God and die." She used an interesting word for *curse*. It's actually the Hebrew word for *bless*—but dripping with sarcasm. She's saying, "Sure, bless God and die." She's blaming God.

But Job didn't. He said she's acting like a foolish woman. The word *foolish* basically means "stupidly seeing life only from *your* perspective."

But notice: Job got mad. In fact, in his anger he shaked his fist in the face of God and questioned him. But when Job asked God hard questions, he wasn't blaming God. The difference was that in his anger, he understood that God allows the good and the bad.

When we're in pain, we might ask God tough questions and cry out to him. Jesus himself cried out to God when he was about to be crucified. Crying out to God *is* acknowledging God. It's okay to acknowledge. That was the difference between Job and his wife. Job acknowledged—his wife blamed.

What do you do when tough times come your way? Do you blame God or turn to God for help?

At the end of the book of Job, God spoke (chapters 38-42). It's a wonderful conversation where God reveals himself and his creative power in nature to Job. Job was so overwhelmed that his response was,

> "My ears had heard of you, but now my eyes have
> seen you." (Job 42:5)

What did Job see? God taught Job how to see him in nature. God taught Job how to see him from the huge galaxies to the microscopic parts of the universe. Our own hope isn't found in pat answers to the questions, "Why do we suffer? Why do we experience loss?" Our hope is in God, the Creator of the universe.

CLOSING:

Christians were never promised painless lives. The world is full of pain. What Christians are promised is that God is our hope in the midst of pain, and God will go through it with us.

Francis Schaeffer argues in his book, *The God Who Is There*, that "you cannot have a personal relationship with something unknown" (p. 144). You have to know that *God is* before you can think about a relationship with God. The beginning of the good news is that *God is there*. God exists. Job learned that lesson. Lisa learned that lesson. She didn't blame God; she turned to God for help, committing her life to him.

Sample Prayer: *God, help me to pray like Job, "I've heard of you before, but now I see you" Help me in my questions and anger and pain to find hope in you and your love. Help me to focus not on what you do for me but on your presence. Help me to see you as Job saw you.*

TALK 24
TITLE: RUNNING HOME

TOPIC: God's Love for Us

BIG IDEA: God just wants us to come home.

SCRIPTURE:

> "So he got up and went to his father. But while he was still a long way off, his father saw him and was filled with compassion for him; he ran to his son, threw his arms around him and kissed him." (Luke 15:20)

PARTICULARS:

I stole this story from the Bible. Some of you might recognize this modern-day version of the prodigal son from my second book, *Do They Run When They See You Coming?* This story is one that could go very long. It can be done in 10 minutes, but you'll want to rehearse it to keep it short. I've filled 30-minute slots with versions of this talk.

THE STORY:

Everett Mann had a great relationship with his father while grow-ing up. His father loved him deeply and always told him so. Everett and his older brother always played together with their father.

Everett particularly liked baseball. As he grew up, one of his favorite times was playing catch with his father. They laughed and talked, and Everett's dad always affirmed him in everything he did. This was weird to Everett's little friends, because their dads weren't like this. You see, Everett lived in an extremely wealthy area of Santa Barbara. Most of Everett's friends were also wealthy. Their fathers unfortunately worked late into the night and traveled for weeks at a time. Their fathers didn't play with them often, and the words they exchanged when they were home weren't always positive.

As Everett grew up he began to play baseball at school. As games and practice took more and more of Everett's time, Ever-ett's dad saw less and less of him. But at every single game, Ever-ett could look into the bleachers just above the first-base line, and his dad was there, cheering the loudest, smiling the biggest. Here and there on a Saturday, Everett and his father would play catch or go to breakfast together, but those times started fading as Everett spent more and more time with his friends.

At first, Everett's time with his friends was innocent, usually playing baseball or just goofing around. But in high school, Ever-ett's friends went to parties on Friday and Saturday nights. Everett went, but he wouldn't drink or do anything stupid. He just liked hanging out with his friends. Everett's dad would often grab his mitt and say, "Do you want to play catch?"

"No thanks, Dad, I gotta go to Michael's house."

Something happened. The more Everett went to parties on Friday and Saturday night, the more he wanted to sleep in late on Saturday and Sunday. Sunday had always been the day he and his father spent together. Everett often slept past noon on Sundays and then went to hang out with his friends. Everett's father finally mentioned something to him. "Everett, you know I love you, and I want the best for you—but I'm worried. You're getting in at 2 and 3 a.m. I can't have that in this house. You know I have a midnight curfew for you, for your protection."

"Dad, Michael's dad lets him stay out as late as he wants."

"That's not the point."

"That's entirely the point. You have too many rules."

"Everett. I love you. I don't want you doing something that will hurt you."

"I can take care of myself!"

Everett's father paused and looked down. "Everett, what about our time on Sundays? I miss that time. Last week I had Dodgers tickets, and you didn't even want to go to the game with me. What's wrong?"

"Nothing's wrong. I just want to live my own life."

"Everett, you know I'm here for you. I can help you if you're getting into trouble."

"I'm not getting in trouble, Dad. Just back off, okay?" Everett was lying. He was a senior now, and he was starting to do things with his friends he knew he shouldn't do. He got good at hiding these things from his father. He got good at hiding these things from himself.

When Everett graduated from high school, he'd already decided the path for his life. He decided he didn't want to do the college thing as his brother had done. Everett wanted to go live with his friends on the beach. After sleeping in until 1:30 in the afternoon the Saturday after his big graduation party, he told his dad.

"Dad, I know you're not gonna like it, and I don't want a lecture, but I'm not going to college."

His father was silent.

"I know you probably want me to be more like my brother..."

"Everett, I never wanted you to be anything..."

"Dad! Save it! I'm taking the money in the account you set up for me and going to live with Michael and the other guys. Don't try to stop me."

Everett had prepared himself for a fight, for yelling and screaming. There wasn't any. He didn't want to stay, so he grabbed his bags and left. As the door slammed, Everett didn't hear his father begin to weep.

Everett got a condo on the beach a little bit north of his home, out by the city college. If you went to that school, you knew who

Everett was, because every Friday and Saturday night the biggest parties were there.

Everett's bank account wasn't small. He had the right clothes, the right cars, the right place, and the wrong friends. He partied for years. He didn't go to school, didn't get a job, just partied.

One day years later, Everett was in Macy's buying a leather jacket. He tossed the cashier his credit card and tapped his fingers impatiently, waiting for the cashier, who was taking entirely too long. Finally the cashier spoke up.

"Mr. Mann, I'm sorry, but your card won't go through."

"That's impossible!"

"I tried it two times. Do you have another one?"

Everett tried card after card and got the same response. Finally he left the jacket with the flustered cashier and walked outside, turning on his cell phone and speed-dialing his accountant. His calls wouldn't go through, so he drove across the parking lot to a pay phone.

"Jake! What's up?! I'm trying to buy a jacket and none of my cards are going through!"

"Everett, I've been trying to reach you, but your cell service is off!"

"What's up with that? What do I pay you for?"

"That's the point, Everett. You haven't paid me in three months.

I've been trying to tell you to stop spending—you're broke!"

"Well, transfer some stocks into the money market."

"That's what you've been telling me, and I've been doing it for months. Everett! Listen to me! There's nothing left!"

Two weeks later Everett's condo had a white piece of paper on the door. He had 30 days to get out. By now his friends were long gone—they'd left when the money left, and Everett started selling things.

Months later, Everett was walking down the street with everything he owned in a small backpack. With no car, no place to live, and no friends, Everett made his way down Highway 101 with his thumb out.

He got a ride down to Carpenteria, where he was let off near some avocado farms. Everett didn't know where he was, or where he was going, for that matter. He saw a farmhouse off in the distance and thought it was worth a try. He walked up a long driveway leading to a small stucco house with a big front porch and one of those wooden porch swings. He rang the doorbell and stood there waiting. When he rang the doorbell, Everett felt worse than he'd ever felt in his entire life. He'd left his family, squandered his money, wasted his life, and now he had to resort to asking for help. Ringing the doorbell was an admission of this fact.

The door was finally opened by a large man wearing a flannel shirt and jeans that were unbuttoned in the front. He looked Everett over from head to toe and barked, "Can I help you with something?"

"I don't know," Everett said, confused by what he was even doing there. "I guess I wondered if you had a place to stay, or knew of a place I could stay—and work, of course."

"Well, ain't this a kick in the pants. I just let somebody go Monday. You ever picked avocados?"

Everett lied. "Yeah—a little bit." He knew just how to choose them at the store down the street from his place. He made a mean guacamole dip.

"Follow me." The man took him around the house to a barn-like building in the back. There were a few animals back there, and an old Mitsubishi 4x4 that had seen better days. They hopped in the 4x4 and Everett was given a tour of the place. The man showed him a place in the loft where Everett could stay. Before he knew what had happened, Everett was picking avocados by day and shoveling horse and pig manure at night.

The job was fine for a couple of weeks. Everett had never worked with his hands, but he'd always kept in good shape for baseball. He learned how to pick avocados soon enough to cover his bluff, and anyone could feed and clean up after horses and pigs.

One day Everett sat on a fence watching the pigs eat the leftovers of the farmer's dinner. As Everett stared down at the cornbread, he found himself getting hungry. The thought crossed his mind that he could grab that piece of cornbread out of the pigs' trough, but as soon as the thought entered his mind, he got mad. *I can't believe I'm sitting here feeding pigs, thinking about eating their food.* Everett looked at his hands. *Look at my hands. They're all cut and callused. And I sleep in a barn! Even my father's servants eat bet-*

ter and live in the guest house. Everett came to his senses. *What am I doing here?*

Everett grabbed his small backpack, and without saying goodbye he left down the long driveway. He made his way to the main road, stuck his thumb out, and started toward home. He didn't know if his father was still there, or if he'd even take Everett back, but he figured it was worth a try.

A mile down the 101 a semi picked him up. Everett rehearsed what he'd say to his father when he saw him. "Dad, I know I turned my back on you. But I want you to take me back..."

He knew that wasn't the right approach. "Dad, I know I turned my back on you, and you probably don't want me as your son. But maybe you would accept me as your servant..."

The truck slowed down and let him out by the old shopping center. He walked up the hill, noticing his tattered clothes and the holes in his shoes. This was the first time in his life he wasn't dressed in the best of clothes.

Thunder clapped after a flash of lighting illuminated the dark redwoods reaching up to the sky. Within a minute rain began its rhythmic patter on the curvy road. Everett pulled his torn jacket up over his head and rounded the corner into his cul-de-sac.

He was having second thoughts. Now that he was just a few steps from his old home, regret and fear began to overwhelm him. But the curiosity of the moment kept his feet moving forward. After all, he didn't even know if his father still lived here.

As he approached the old house, Everett noticed how different it looked. The trees were much taller, and the house was a different color. Everett stopped and stared for a moment, then caught sight of the mailbox out by the edge of the driveway. Glancing around, he slowly approached the mailbox and opened it up. A few pieces of mail were tucked safe and dry inside the box. Everett pulled the top letter out with his callused hand and read the name of the recipient.

He didn't know whether to sigh in relief or to turn around and run away. Years of seeking fulfillment on his own had led him nowhere. His father had been right and Everett had been wrong. And here he was, back at his father's doorstep, broke, dirty, shameful—a failure.

The name on the envelope was his father's. There was no avoiding it—this was his father's house. But as Everett slipped the letter back in the mailbox, he knew he didn't have the courage to knock on the door and face ultimate humiliation.

Everett's finger brushed against something sticky on the lid of the mailbox. An old piece of paper was attached to the lid with an old piece of masking tape. On the tape was a smear of ink that had faded from years of weathering. Everett peered closely at the smudge of ink, trying to make out the faded word. He swallowed when he saw it. The word was "Everett."

He grabbed the tape, which pulled easily from the lid of the box. The old piece of paper was folded into small squares and almost fell apart as Everett opened it. It was a letter from his father.

Dear Everett,

Welcome home, my son. There's food in the refrigerator. There are blankets in the closet. I kept your room for you just the way you left it.

The key is hidden where it always was.

Welcome home, son.

I love you,

Daddy

The rain dripping from Everett's hair camouflaged the tears streaming from his eyes. He slammed the mailbox shut and started to throw the note to the ground—but he couldn't bear to part with it. So he shoved the note in his pocket and turned toward the main road.

The sky had darkened now, so Everett was able to see the headlights coming from the main road. He ducked behind the neighbor's front bushes. He was sure his present appearance wasn't a welcome one, and he didn't feel like answering questions.

A car he didn't recognize pulled into the driveway of his old house. He kept his head low, peering through the wet leaves of the neighbor's shrubs.

A man stepped out of the car, gathered his things, and shut the car door. He started to head into the house, but stopped and turned toward the mailbox.

Everett stayed low and strained to see man's face silhouetted against the sky.

The man approached the mailbox and opened the door, pulling out the mail. As the man turned to face the box, Everett recognized his face.

His father had aged quite a bit. His gray hair was thin and combed neatly back behind his ears. His kind eyes scanned the mail quickly, not satisfied with what they saw. But then his father froze for a few seconds that seemed like an eternity to Everett. His father rubbed his thumb against the empty spot on the mailbox lid, finally shutting the lid and scanning the street for a sign of movement. His eyebrows were raised and his eyes full of hope.

He tucked his mail with his other papers and moved quickly toward the front door. Everett stayed low, his legs cramping from squatting so long. His feet were in topsoil and there was no place to sit.

As his father disappeared into the house, Everett started to get up from his cramped position. As he took a few steps out into the open, the house lights came on and the big driveway light shone down the street. Everett didn't move as he saw his dad go to the front window and peer outside.

Everett was in plain view. He didn't move. He figured his father wouldn't recognize him. But his father stared intently through the window. Across the street and through the rain, Everett stared into the eyes of the old man behind the large pane of glass. The kind eyes saw beyond the dirt and wear on Everett's face and lit up with excitement.

Before he could move, his father ran to the front door, flung it open, and ran through the rain toward him.

Everett didn't know what to do. He stood there for a second before remembering the speech he rehearsed.

But it was more that he could bear. His father ran beyond the ability of a man that age. His arms were outstretched and his eyes flooded with tears. As his father caught him, Everett fell into his arms. Tears burst from his eyes and he couldn't hold back the sobs of anguish. Everett was cradled in his father's arms, enjoying a feeling he hadn't felt in years—a hug from his daddy.

His father bellowed, "Everett, my son. You've come home! Welcome home, my son!"

Everett tried to get out the words he'd rehearsed, but his father wouldn't have any of it. He grabbed Everett's head and buried it in his chest and held him tighter than Everett had ever been held before.

"I don't care where you've been, I don't care what you've done, I'm just glad you're home. Welcome home, my son."

TRANSITION STATEMENT:

Wouldn't you like to hear those words?

God is waiting to tell you those words right now.

APPLICATION AND SCRIPTURE:

This story is just a ripoff of the powerful story of the prodigal son that Jesus tells in the Bible in Luke 15. Jesus wanted to paint a picture of what God was like and give us a glimpse of how much he loves us.

God is, of course, sad that we've run away. And God just wants us to return home. Jesus told us the story of a young man who turned his back on his father and left. But the father didn't hold it against him. Listen to Jesus' exact words in Luke 15:20: "So he [the young man] got up and went to his father. But while he was still a long way off, his father saw him and was filled with compassion for him; he ran to his son, threw his arms around him and kissed him."

God's arms are open wide; God wants you to come home.

CLOSING:

I want you to close your eyes right now as I pray. As you close your eyes, I want you to think about something:

1. Many of you have run away from God and lived life your own way rather than God's way.

2. Some of you have even hit rock bottom as the young man in the story did. The partying ended, and he realized he was empty.

3. Right now some of you might even be like Everett who finally came to his senses and realized that he had it much better in the relationship with his father.

Now it's time to come home to him. Pray with me now: *Father, I've run away from you. And I've realized that life without you is meaningless. I want to give up that life and return home to you right now. Amen.*

Source: *Do They Run When They See You Coming?* Youth Specialties, 2004